MANAGEMENT AND
THE AUDIT NETWORK

THE WILEY–INSTITUTE OF INTERNAL AUDITORS PROFESSIONAL BOOK SERIES

Gill Courtemanche • The New Internal Auditing
Philip Kropatkin • Management and the Audit
Network

MANAGEMENT AND THE AUDIT NETWORK

Internal Auditors, CPAs, and the CEO

Philip Kropatkin

JOHN WILEY & SONS

New York • Chichester • Brisbane • Toronto • Singapore

Copyright © 1987 by John Wiley & Sons, Inc.

All rights reserved. Published simultaneously in Canada.

Reproduction or translation of any part of this work
beyond that permitted by Section 107 or 108 of the
1976 United States Copyright Act without the permission
of the copyright owner is unlawful. Requests for
permission or further information should be addressed to
the Permissions Department. John Wiley & Sons, Inc.

This publication is designed to provide accurate and
authoritative information in regard to the subject
matter covered. It is sold with the understanding that
the publisher is not engaged in rendering legal, accounting,
or other professional service. If legal advice or other
expert assistance is required, the services of a competent
professional person should be sought. *From a Declaration
of Principles jointly adopted by a Committee of the
American Bar Association and a Committee of Publishers.*

Library of Congress Cataloging in Publication Data:

Kropatkin, Philip.
  Management and the audit network.
(The Wiley/Ronald Institute of Internal Auditors professional
book series)
  Bibliography: p.
  1. Auditing. I. Title. II. Series.
HF5667.K74 1987   657'.45   86-33983
ISBN 0-471-83286-3

Printed in the United States of America

10 9 8 7 6 5 4 3 2 1

Preface

This book represented a real challenge: how to write a text that combines practicality and advanced concepts and that illustrates the benefits accruable to an organization in which the whole audit network (staff accountants, external CPAs, and internal auditors) is understood and embraced as an important adjunct to the upper management team, especially the chief executive officer. These men and women of the audit network are often engulfed in conflicting pressures arising from the particular concerns of different departments within the organization.

Furthermore, this book is an ambitious attempt to describe the importance of organizational practices, patterns, and attitudes as key signals for the network people if they want to be of real assistance to their managers. These signals are of the utmost importance in sensing vulnerabilities and in determining whether critical internal controls are really working. Stated otherwise, for managers to be able to be at their best, they must know who their network people are, what they do, and how they do it (in some detail); they must "dig in and orchestrate" the network's performance to show their leadership abilities.

On the other hand, an important responsibility for auditors and accountants is to be able to absorb intellectually what their CEOs are driving at (corporate objectives), and to coordinate expeditiously their own staff's efforts with all other relevant professionals to achieve the best overall results!

Using my rather unique experience of forty-odd years of auditing everything from small businesses to billion dollar programs, with activities ranging from individualized "grunt" work (checking expenses and balance sheet items) to managing a staff of over 1000 professionals with a budget of over $40 million, and consulting with clients and academia, I have strived to ferret out common denominators and useful practical concepts that work in the real world. Therefore, with analytical skills constantly being challenged and honed by perceptive colleagues, I have attempted to put together, in one easy-to-read narrative with no distracting detail or extended samples, a composite view and a set of interesting suggestions as to how the whole managerial/auditing network can benefit from mutually enhanced understanding.

Auditors must stop talking only to other auditors. Managers have to be more involved in, and consult with, the inner workings of the professional network. Middle managers' analyses and insights can be as useful as those of the CEOs' trusted staff assistants and top line managers. I have rarely, if ever, seen a top official at a professional auditing or managerial accounting seminar.

In our modern business world, an increasingly complicated and vulnerable arena, a "vector of forces" constantly swirls around the CEO. Meaningful movement by the CEO in the vortex of this whirlpool depends to a great degree on detailed knowledge and logical insights as to how this network operates.

PHILIP KROPATKIN

Mill Creek, Washington
April 1987

Acknowledgment

I wish to thank my friend and colleague, Charles L. Johnson, for his great help and perceptive counsel in reviewing and editing this book.

P.K.

Contents

MANAGEMENT AND THE AUDIT NETWORK

1

Introduction

OVERVIEW

Top managers, chief executive officers (CEOs), and the like face unrelenting pressures on their time and talents. Decisions must be swift and sure. The CEO's ability to deflect and control these pressures will determine the quality of the company's performance.

With this premise as a theme, I began thinking of the particular insights I, as a former chief auditor, might share with CEOs to help them better manage themselves and their subordinates. There are important truths that the manager must learn—and live. This book relates many that I have learned in 40 years of professional and managerial experience.

Underlying all the concepts I'll discuss is my one basic theory: CEOs are forever caught in a whirlpool of conflicting—sometimes harsh—demands and forces. I call these forces the "swirling currents" of daily life in the executive's office.

These forces can be changed, tamed, and harnessed to serve the organization. And one of the best ways for CEOs to do this is to understand and use the professionals who work for and represent them—their "network" of experts.

Here is where one of the basic truths emerges. The people who form a company's management support network are paid by *the company* for their services, whether they are company employees or consultants hired on an as-needed basis. It is the CEO's *right* and *obligation* to see that full value is received for dollars spent. In fact, *only* the CEO is capable of orchestrating the network.

In this book I deal mainly with the stars of this network—the accountants and auditors—because of their unique position within the organization's structure. Consider: Accountants gather and format data. They translate the meaning of these data. They review and appraise how all the information is hung together. Accountants and auditors are—or certainly ought to be—in a unique position to view the entire organization *from within*. Like a skilled mechanic under the hood, the good network serves to identify and recommend everything from fine tuning—minor tweaks and adjustments—to major repairs.

Last, the network may then attest to outsiders how reliable it all is. Who then can deny the substantive and widespread influence of accountants, or their ability to help the CEO identify and harness the swirling currents that challenge a company's stability.

Chief executive officers take many forms: business owners struggling to stay alive and prosper; heads of government agencies shackled with the problems of government while trying to get their jobs done; executive heads of major corporations, profit and not-for-profit. Whatever form they take, they all have one thing in common: a network, often "untidy," of professionals on whom they rely.

No matter how big or small are the companies they manage, all CEOs face a similar challenge: to avoid serious error, or deliberate wrongdoing, in the management of their organizations. Thus it falls to the people in control—particularly the CEO—to get the network working, and working well; to harness all the best forces and most innovative and expert techniques available; and to *find* the best people, *hire* them, and get them closely aligned and planning together.

Perhaps the reason the network's potential hasn't been explored and exploited in the average organization is a reluctance to question professionals at their work, even the view by the "generalist" executive that the professionals' work is so specialized, so arcane, that it is beyond comprehension.

This book is a primer for that CEO who wants to assemble and use the network to the company's best advantage. It will uncloak the mysteries of the accountants' and auditors' roles within the network and deliver concise, concrete methods for better executive management.

THE BASIC MESSAGE

Business today can be described in many ways: complex, computerized, depersonalized, and vulnerable. Like a sea, it can appear calm from a distance, but upon closer inspection reveal turbulence just below the surface—the swirling currents that challenge the CEO's skill, strength, endurance, and sense of direction.

Four of these swirling currents, or forces, are:

1. Internal Forces. From the organization's owners, constituents, and/or stockholders, who relentlessly press for greater profits (through increased sales or reduced costs); and for better returns (through greater productivity and efficiency).

2. External Forces. From a whole assault team of government regulatory and taxing agencies; professional associations and their related formal societies; legal, judicial, and community pressures; special interest groups, competitors, and customers.

3. Conceptual Forces. The audit process is plagued with ever-increasing accounting and auditing uncertainties (and disparities). The manager must sort out: what is material (it seems to vary from manager to manager); what is reasonably controllable (that which makes for effective internal control is widely debated and often underestimated. Yearly losses of $200 billion from fraud and abuse attest to this. Also, there is the challenge of making audits profitable without violating standards, standards that often call for heavy and time-consuming procedures. Finally, the manager must determine what is *effective*, and how to get a reasonable fix on this complicated, analytical task.

4. Mechanical Forces. From the dramatic and ongoing explosion of computers and computerized data, accompanied by the worrisome use of electronic transfer mechanisms. These make it difficult to fix precise responsibility for error. Tabulated, ledgerlike accounts are mostly unavailable for retrospective analysis or audit, and only a series of current ending balances is easily studied.

Furthermore, managers are now captives of the computer printout age and victims of the now-common malady, "spreadsheetitis." Many are also infected with the insidious "Xerox urge," where they feel naked without a copy of everything. These place a heavy burden on conscientious managers. The daily accumulation of information (with the important frequently mingled with the trivial) can overwhelm the executive.

First-line supervisors, even those with fantastic memories, are often intimidated. They regard this deluge of data as "homework" they may be called on to recite. It surely inhibits their ability to devote sufficient time to organizational horizon-broadening, or to engage in productive and logical thinking, or to pay attention, for the most part, to each day's higher priority items.

With all these forces at work, a good network becomes of prime importance to the CEO. And the network can only work as responsively, effectively, and efficiently as the CEO permits. In other words, it is up to the CEO to design the network and lay the groundwork. In the following, the three major bricks in the foundation of any solid network are discussed. The CEO must recognize the importance of each, and then must put each in place before the structure can be built.

1. A Blueprint of the Network Structure. Sort out, and obtain a clearer understanding of the network participants and how they interact, then depict it in a concise organizational chart.

Knowledge of what drives an organization, or what immobilizes it, is more accessible if the structure is clearly defined and simply depicted. A chart (Figure 1) on page 26 graphically illustrates how an organization can move its forces into a single alignment to instigate action in a desired direction.

2. *The Right Data, When You Need It.* Historically, accountants and auditors tend to do their own thing, guided by their own formally prescribed standards, set by their state and national societies. While CEOs should not tinker with the prescribed standards, they should require of their professional technicians concise reports, delivered on schedule.

However, this might not be an easy task. Many professionals hide behind a shield of accumulated knowledge and expertise, a shield their generalist managers are hesitant to penetrate. But penetrate you must, and take charge of this team and the information it delivers.

3. *Judicious Use of the "Executive Override."* The professional network is extremely sensitive to management attitudes and actions that appear contrary to the original purpose. Even the tightest system of internal controls set in place by expert accountants—with the understanding and approval of executive management—falls prey to override actions by the CEO who supervised its construction. The latest and best accounting techniques lose their significance if the CEOs seek their "own" data from another source. Design and build right from the beginning, and you'll minimize the need to tinker with the machinery.

ORGANIZATIONAL STYLE

Many training courses and texts call for an examination of the business *systems* of an organization to forge an understanding of its controls. This comfortable old practice, however, is no longer penetrating enough. It is equally important—perhaps of paramount importance—to get a grip on an organization's *style* as it is to be familiar with its business cycles and record-keeping techniques before considering or creating its controls.

What are the components of organizational style? They include management psychology, executive attitudes, corporate culture, the philosophies behind the company's creation, and the way the organization responds to internal and external forces.

What then really brings a company into being? What makes it productive, profitable, and controllable? And how can its performance best be managed, evaluated, audited, or attested? We can't answer this last question without examining the answers to the first two.

An organization does not start with a product, or a manufacturing facility. Nor does it begin with a service and a built-in delivery system. Businesses are begun by *people*—entrepreneurs with ideas, vision, and, usually, high motivation. Venture capital and assets come later.

Furthermore, a company doesn't charge out of the starting gates assured of a first-place finish. First, it must develop a strong management team that in turn can build a stable work force to make and sell its product. And, what is very important, the real managerial superstars know how to take the progressive forces (administrative ethical behavior) behind a well-run organization, and duplicate them throughout the system.

In the background is an organizational style, for better or worse, set in motion by the CEOs or owners. The "superchiefs" instinctively know how to make *people*—throughout the company—deliver their best, knowing they will be recognized and rewarded for their efforts. These are the powerful inner thrusts that, all else being equal, usually determine how controllable, innovative—and profitable—an organization will be over the long haul.

THE UNTIDY NETWORK

Finally, there is the CEO's network, a changing cast of players that must be directed by the executive for maximum effect. But what makes this network hard to harness is its variety and potency, its relative independence of the company's operating groups, and its inward attention to its own methods and agendas.

This network includes accountants, auditors, lawyers, professors, engineers, investigators, ADP professionals, human resources consultants, contracting and purchasing officers, security, insurance and financial management specialists, and so on. And each profession has its own set of standards, industry norms, and certification programs administered by its various professional societies, dictating ethics and methods *within the CEO's organization!*

The audit part of the network is its most fascinating segment. Running an auditing function involves managing one's own staff, with the purpose of helping the company's other managers better run their own departments, divisions, and staffs. This is known as the *audit recommendation process.*

THE WHOLE BODY APPROACH

Just as medical professionals today are taking a holistic approach to the human body, looking at more than the physical symptoms but at the emotional and environmental factors that influence the body as well, accountants and auditors are often in the unique position to view the entire company as one organism—from within. They see how all its organs and systems function individually and how each relates to the whole. Often, they are aware before anyone else of a disease or malfunction of one system and can prescribe a cure for the affected part that won't disturb the rest.

This holistic approach is the best way to keep the organization in shape, preventively and correctively. Studying budget increases or decreases as a separable exercise, for instance, may be unproductive as a way of viewing discrete administrative needs. It must be tied into the entire company's situation.

Consider the following "balloon analogy." Picture an organization as a balloon containing a fixed volume (of expenses) within it. If there is no "open neck" to the full budget and you press for efficiencies at one end by pushing in the balloon, the total volume remains the same. It merely changes form and bulges out elsewhere.

This is where the network's understanding of the workings of the whole organization—its systems *and* style—serves the CEO. And that is why the person occupying the executive office must understand and communicate with the company's audit network.

2

The Network and Its Swirling Currents

In Part One, CEOs and business owners were depicted in a vortex, surrounded by forces—external, internal, conceptual, and even mechanical (computers and the information age)—that make up the swirling currents of daily life in the executive's office. The following list, while not all inclusive, includes many common pressure points:

Factors relating to profit motivators

Regulatory agency demands and restrictions

Keeping up with computer technology, capabilities and cost considerations

Client or customer litigation potential

ADP environment and security concerns

Staff training requirements versus shrinking budgets

IRS prescriptions and changing tax structures

Credit institutions and banking rules

Employee drug and alcohol abuse

Accounting and audit considerations and strictures imposed
by various professional societies

The materiality problem: what to control and at what cost.

THE INTERNAL/EXTERNAL AUDIT NETWORK

Chief executive officers work with two main groups of accountants: those who keep the company's books and those who check
on how well the books are kept, the auditors. The auditors in
turn are subdivided as follows:

Internal. Those on the company's payroll and under executive
management's direct supervision.

External. Those hired for specific situations and purposes but
who are not reportable to the CEO in a staff or administrative sense.

Let us now consider the combination of potent forces, so useful
to the CEO in harnessing and controlling the others.

1. The First Point. A closely woven network of internal and
external auditors, properly understood and coordinated, can
be a real boon to the harried manager.

2. The Second Point. First, a CEO must appreciate that this
network, too, has its own set of swirling currents—events that
affect it—which must be appreciated and understood before
the network can be used properly. Again, only the CEO can
orchestrate this work.

3. The Third Point. In addition to the quality of audit work,
the CEO's *attitude* is the absolute keystone of reliable internal
controls and organizational excellence. Top management truly
sets the *accepted patterns* so vital throughout the organization
for ethical and profitable operations. But, senior executives,
operating managers, and accounting staff often view their
relationships with internal and external auditors with uncer-

tainty. They generally do not understand exactly how the auditors operate, just what standards and constraints they face, and how they can do more than they do now. What follows will help to define this network.

Independent External Auditors

These certifiers of management's reports are contracted by management to assure the company's stockholders, lenders, and the general public that company books and records accurately represent the assets and liabilities of the company as of a particular date. The external auditors also certify that all figures were compiled in a manner consistent with previous periods (or that any deviations are explained in the report, such as changing to an installment method of accounting).

The general rule is not to deceive the reader in any material fashion. External auditors do not portray the financial condition of their clients, but rather verify the accuracy of their statements.

Independent external auditors are engaged by plaintiffs whose legal action calls for an opinion independent of the firm in any manner. In other instances, the law requires that an independent audit firm certify the accuracy of a company's recorded statements, such as with SEC-approved publicly held entities, or as regards the "single audit" needs of government grantees.

The work of independent auditors includes the testing of internal controls within an organization; and by special arrangement may include systems analyses, industry-based consultation, and the like.

An important network point: External auditors do not make sufficient use of internal audit staffs or of in-house accounting or physical asset (inventory and warehouse) specialists. They tend to go it alone. This is neither cost-effective nor reliable. Timeliness of testing is a key ingredient of accuracy and control, and on-site personnel can assist in the examinations (with proper supervision). CPAs often view such an alliance as a loss of independence, or status, or billable time. Wrong! The standards of the accounting profession encourage the use of any corroborative measures. This creates better profitable audits and permits full scope audits that otherwise might have been restricted by cost considerations.

Internal Auditors

These individuals, working within and employed by an organization, check on its internal controls and weak spots. Some believe they are an intrinsic part of the internal control mechanisms. Others feel their primary role takes them technically outside of the mechanism itself to better assess its reliability. It makes sense to leave both options open, depending on what particular situations require. If, for example, one area is weak on controlling its operations, it might be necessary—even urgent—for the internal auditors to step in and help restore controls. Once they have the controls working again, the auditors can stay clear except for periodic checking to make sure the controls are still in force.

In any event, the auditors' "independence" stems primarily from their own professional standards, and that independence is buttressed by the support of the CEO, and that office's insistence that the auditors be allowed to do their work, unfettered by preconceptions or organizational prejudices. When the auditors' examination is complete and recommendations penned, they need feedback, affirmation and action by the CEO to make the needed changes.

The Internal Auditor's Work Includes:

Reporting on the accuracy of in-house data and operating records

Testing the safeguards over assets, electronic data, and other sensitive materials

Looking for ways to improve economy and efficiency. The auditors' recommendations frequently more than pay for their cost. A related task—reviewing program effectiveness—calls for the best in renaissance auditors. This service is used by perceptive CEOs who want to avoid getting better and better at doing the wrong thing.

Providing *on-line* (current) testing and sampling of data so that operations managers have a reliable basis for making decisions. Nothing could be more important. The auditors' ability to be on the scene daily and aware of corporate concerns and directions is a definite plus. External auditors are then able to feel more secure in their periodic attest duties.

Internal auditors perform under the standards set by the Institute of Internal Auditors (IIA), which standards are compatible with those set by the General Accounting Office (GAO) and the American Institute of Certified Public Accountants (AICPA). All three set basically the same requirements for education, training, supervision, planning, and, as mentioned before, independence in attitude.

Fortunately, internal auditors are not yet encumbered by an unmanageable set of special considerations and interpretations—the "standards overload syndrome" that many independent professionals descry. However, because the IIA's standards are so similar to those of the GAO and the AICPA, CEOs should insist their internal audit functions be set up to work smoothly with external auditors and their standards. This allows better audit coverage, which in turn affords better protection and cost savings.

Professional Societies

The societies that serve the accounting professions, including the IIA and the AICPA and all state societies, set the standards, write policy, and establish continuing education requirements. (In the views of many theorists and practitioners, there exists a serious standards overload which unnecessarily burdens accountants with smaller, more generalized, private practices. They argue that the smaller practitioners work so closely with their clients and are so familiar with their operations and controls that they can satisfy the requirements of professional expertise with a more limited set of rules and specifications.)

The Professional Societies:

Operate certification programs, which award accreditation as certified public accountant, certified internal auditor, and the like

Work closely with legislative and regulatory bodies, including the Securities and Exchange Commission (SEC), the GAO, the Office of Management and the Budget (OMB), as well as various, concerned Congressional oversight committees.

Publish and encourage publication of texts, articles, research papers, and policy statements.

Conduct or sponsor training sessions and seminars. Notably, these evidence a concentration on tax matters and tough speciality subjects like real estate, bankruptcy, construction, and so on. They rarely address topics fundamental to the profession like ethics; the essence (attitude) of organization controls; the desirability, if not the absolute urgency, of a broad liberal arts background for auditors; and the fraud responsibilities of auditors.

Academe and Its Impact on Network Players

As discussed here, academe consists of the formal teachers of the network participants. They are also the researchers into new methods and the questioners of older methods. They might be considered the overseers of, and intellectual commentators on, the profession from a scholarly, historical point of view.

It is fair to say (and its members might be the first to admit) that academe is the most difficult group in the network to categorize and describe. The primary objective of the teachers and trainers—and the professional societies that prescribe continuing educational requirements—should be to prepare auditors for their varied roles in an increasingly diverse corporate world.

Accordingly, an accountant's (auditor's) education should include:

Writing Skills. This ability is unchallenged for the number one spot. What good is an audit effort if it is not described in concise, clear, and actionable terms? Good writing skills set professionals apart more than anything else. All else being equal, the good communicators will move ahead faster than their peers.

Interviewing and Observation Skills. Auditors must be able to spot items that just don't fit. The standards recognize this. They warn, in very stern terms, that auditors must do *whatever is necessary to avoid overlooking gross misapplications.*

Any Number of Liberal Arts Skills. A generous dash of humanities education will help the practitioner understand all parts of a complex organization—from the laborer on the shop floor to the graphic artist. Audits deal with more than numbers, and recommendations are made always to *people.*

Technical Education. The obvious skills of the debit and credit world.

Overall, what is of concern to every working professional, and to the managers of newly educated auditors, is that few can function reliably and usefully on the "audit logic" level when they enter the marketplace. They cannot write well because they cannot think well. They have not been pressed to understand the meaning of things—what is trivial versus what is material.

Wish List for Academic Improvement

Following is an agenda for professional/academic realignment:

More exchange of ideas and the identification of discrete needs between (1) CEOs and executive practitioners; and (2) professors and their deans and trustees.

Awareness that many of the best and most quickly filled courses are developed and taught by nonprofit foundations, professional societies, private companies and individual consultants—not by academe.

Increase in corporate training budgets for accounting professionals. Training is usually regarded as an easily eliminated overhead expense or perk. All too often, the staff
members sent to seminars and workshops are not the key
people in the organization, but the most dispensable.

Making CEOs aware that participation is conceptual, as well
as practical, seminars can be a present need for them and
their subordinates.

Increasing the number of colleges and universities that offer
an active, and full, audit study program—or even one with
current and advanced techniques courses.

To sum up. Academe should be recruiting high-level, thinking practitioners who know how to stimulate and prepare a
new breed of renaissance auditors capable of outstanding performance within and without the audit network.

BASIC CONCERNS

To this point, we have presented an overview of the audit community. We have described its participants, the independent
external auditors and their counterparts inside the organization, and discussed in general terms how professional societies
and the academic world influence their work.

Now we explore why the network does not always function as
well as it could:

*1. The Lack of Real Coordination Between the External and
Internal Auditors.* They frequently fail to combine their efforts to the best possible advantage. The standards by which
each operates are similar; and the expertise is generally equal.
What is needed is top management's insistence that the auditors perform as a team for the best and most cost-effective
results.

2. Continuing Problems with Internal Controls. Internal controls are the means used by an organization to secure its as-

sets and get reliable data for its reports. However, within most companies—and among members of the accounting profession at large—there continues to be disagreement as to what these controls are and how they really function. The solution to this argument in any organization rests with top-level management. The CEO's positive attitude, or subversive actions (the override principle), all have a very strong effect on the audit function. Positive attitudes should be reinforced; subversive actions recognized and eliminated.

3. Differing Opinions of Materiality. What is critical to the external auditors in their periodic financial statement attestations may not be material to an internal auditor's on-line examinations into the economy, efficiency, and effectiveness of the organization he works for. However, a wasteful practice—no matter how small in the overall scheme—always hurts the organization. But if it doesn't materially alter the bottom-line figures that the CPA is certifying (and it takes an awful lot to do that where the balance sheet deals with very large figures), then chances are it goes unnoticed and uncorrected, unless the internal audit function is allowed greater influence.

4. Generally Accepted Accounting Principles. These are a collection of written and unwritten standards, rules, policies, and decisions. The extent and variety of these make them difficult to bring into focus. The body of research and recommendations on proper accounting methods continues to grow, obscuring many an organization's attempts to find "the right way."

Accounting techniques also vary widely. Very often, techniques and "generally accepted principles" clash, especially in small business accounting where strong tax incentives encourage "creative" bookkeeping. This is evidenced by the varying treatment of inventories, currency inflation, capital reserves, pension funds, contingent liabilities, depreciation of assets that are overpriced or understated, and so forth. Time and talent are misused when auditors spend hours calculating prepaid items or deferred amounts. That same time and effort would be better spent scrutinizing operations for gross mis-applications.

5. *Computerized Data.* Extreme vigilance is necessary to insure the system is working correctly, that no programming or data processing errors are obscuring reality. Regular (even daily in some situations) testing of computer-generated data is vital to the attestation function. Internal auditors are in a unique position to provide regular validation of this data.

Computers have changed dramatically all previously held notions of organizational vulnerability. Their impact on internal controls should be viewed with great urgency. Pinpointing the source of an inadvertent error is difficult enough; uncovering deliberate misapplications and fraud is nearly impossible without regular and strenuous testing and checking. Because of the potential for severe loss in a short time, nowhere is it more important for internal and external auditors to work as a team, particularly if they were involved in the design of the system. If the system was designed by ADP experts, either in or out of the organization, then they should build in the proper audit trails, as prescribed by the auditors. It falls to the CEO to get the "heads" together—of accounting, auditing, MIS and data-processing departments—to insure a useful and easily monitored system design.

One very useful security technique, "compartmentalization," can reduce the risk of error. Basically, it is the strict separation of duties and responsibilities that pertain to computer equipment and operations. Programmers should have access to the running of the program; operators should not be responsible for "checking" the runs; and regular security checks should be conducted independently by employees outside the computer programming and operations functions. This "cell theory," of course, contains and minimizes each set of possible losses. Here again the CEO's support of the network should take hold—bringing together the diverse talents of the accountants, ADP wizards, security experts, and auditors—to create cells of operations that deter major error, gross misapplications, or fraud.

Other Computer Considerations

Computer record matching, a technique for comparing one set of computer records with related computer data to detect differences for further analysis and study, is a powerful ally. With the increased use of computer data in all areas of operations, this is a practical and potent tool.

Computers raise another question about the auditor's role. Should there be ADP auditors, or general purpose auditors (the "big picture" types), routinely handling computer operations? Because the ADP specialists are proliferating and functioning on their own terms, it falls to the CEO to coordinate effort in this area.

The specter of portable microcomputers looms large. On one hand, they broaden a company's analytical horizons, permitting swift and responsive tabulation of data in the field. But they also increase management's vulnerability by handing would-be abusers a powerful yet subtle weapon.

In spite of the capabilities of computers, there remain many record-keeping functions that should be closely examined to see if computerization is truly necessary. Smaller firms, or compact operations, might do far better with some old-fashioned yet effective "bookkeeping by hand."

I have audited dozens of firms whose no-nonsense bookkeepers sent the invoices out on time, always had the accounts receivable reconciled, filed all the required IRS tax and payroll forms on time, prepared every employee's paycheck with nary a discrepancy, and all without a hard-to-monitor, and usually more expensive, computerized bookkeeping system.

Consider, also, the relatively untapped human brain. Who can really contemplate the billions and billions of separate images (bits, if you like) that it takes just to look out a window and discern the details of trees, leaves, birds in flight, shapes of buildings, roads—endless detail!

It has been estimated that one trip through New York City's Holland Tunnel, for instance, involves more images on the human brain than there are items stored in many of the complex corporate mainframes—one trip through the tunnel! What is also mystifying is how our brain selectively stores bits that it (consciously or otherwise) decides are material and need remembering; or deems are trivial and can be forgotten—at least for the time being. Our brain automatically resists overload. The point is merely that we should not presume that computers, *per se*, are supreme and are always better able to cope with company records than our human bookkeepers. Keep an open mind.

Relationships Between Internal and External Auditors

The two groups are simply not close enough. Although their standards, techniques, education and basic capabilities are similar, their audit programming interactions need substantial reinforcement. Failing to remedy this situation will result in a loss in efficiency and reliability, to the organization as well as to both groups of professionals.

How can you bring the two closer together? Consider the whole body analogy. Like the human body, a business is not just a collection of separate parts, but a system of connected, cooperative elements. All must work in concert for optimum results. Connecting the "head bone to the neck bone" and so on throughout the corporate organism is an administrative imperative.

Training and education should be part of the whole. Management's budgetary support for such network connection is essential for progress.

To assure smooth operations, checklists of *who* does *what* and *when* are a must. Failing to establish such job descriptions can result in nobody taking responsibility for anything.

Benefits of a Better-Coordinated System

Reduced vulnerability of operations and assets. Especially significant in a computer environment, this alone is worth the time and work involved in connecting the network.

Less exposure to legal liability, which is of concern to audit firms of all sizes. In this litigious era, would-be plaintiffs look for "deep pockets" to dig into. Better internal/external audit connections can shield a company against claims of substandard or misleading practices.

Greater assurance that facts are as represented. Public hearings and media investigations question the reliability of "certified" statements. But CEOs who stand on a base of reliable and consistent reporting and checking by their audit network can stand strong against such incursions.

Fewer opportunities for hidden, ongoing fraud and abuse or gross misapplications of funds.

More cost beneficial, profitable, and effective audit assignments—*the bottom line!*

Firming Up the Audit Network

Management should make a full inventory of the whole set of professionals at its command, consider how each operates individually, and how their work can mesh for the corporate good. This list may include:

Internal auditors
External auditors
In-house systems accountants
ADP professionals
Legal advisors
Human resources managers
Security experts
Specialized industry consultants who are members of distinct professions: doctors, dentists, engineers, scientists, and so forth.

Concentrating on accountants and auditors to begin setting up the network, the next steps are:

1. Ask the external auditors to set forth, in advance of each year's engagement, what assistance they will need from the internal auditors, such as monthly analyses and (timely) testing of controls and data. With some adroit planning and co-operation, both groups could agree on and carry out the overlapping verification procedures that are needed. An ensuing exchange of notes and working papers detailing their findings could be very beneficial.

Two logical places to begin such a reciprocal effort would be (1) testing inventory and warehouse operations (with a tie-in to shipping and receiving procedures, maybe even plant issuing controls), and (2) examining payroll and other labor charges. The regular internal audit presence in these areas could prevent irregularities.

2. Spell out, in no uncertain terms, to the in-house accounting staff what data is crucial to management's needs and in what form; how soon after events occur it is needed for good decisions to be made; and that any new or creative accounting techniques be cleared by the CEO's office if they involve material data. This insures that any changes and innovations are consistent with company objectives.

3. Make it clear to all departments just *who* will test the reliability of this information, and *how*. It is surprising how many subdivisions have their own "quality assurance" personnel, generally installed by the section manager to protect that operation (primarily from superiors). This falls under the heading of avoiding adverse "surprises" and always looking good when the CEO comes looking. Such duplication should be carefully examined. It is possible that the specialized knowledge in each department allows swift response to problems and is therefore beneficial. However, potential conflicts and extra expenses should be carefully weighed against such benefits.

4. Determine what minimum testing and verification is required for certification of the organization's statements and reports. Certification, of course, involves attestation as to the accuracy of these reports and a tested and verified belief that all material facts are reflected therein. But it is crucial to remember that these statements show principally what is on

hand and owed, what was spent or received, or what (material) contingency may be coming to pass, without commenting on whether the corporate or agency objectives were achieved.

Certified statements alone should not be enough to satisfy the CEO. They may show the organization to be extremely efficient, but what they don't reveal is whether what the organization is doing is what it is supposed to be doing. Only a well planned and coordinated audit network will help the CEO certify, beyond the tenets of legal certification, that the organization is fulfilling its larger objectives.

5. Send a clear corporate message as to how audit recommendations that are accepted will be acted upon, and on what timetable. This *audit resolution* process is crucial to the success of the entire oversight endeavor. What point is there in allocating resources to see how well things are running if nothing substantial results from good recommendations?

The success of audit resolution hinges sharply on the personal attention from the very top rung of the executive ladder. This experience has been confirmed at many organizations. The CEO alone may be capable of opening up bottlenecks that have baffled lower-level managers or that have been outside their management purview.

6. Determine the audit priorities. What are they, who sets them, and with what managerial consultation and advice? Here again, the CEO must take an active role in determining and reviewing the priorities. After all, top management should have insight into the potential vulnerabilities of the company and where it might benefit from examination by an independent source. The auditor's intuition should be buttressed by the knowledge of the CEO. Such top-management attention and involvement costs little in relation to the benefits accruing from it.

This book is based on one critical premise: That management, whether in business for profit, or serving a nonprofit organization or public constituency, wants to do its best to be efficient and effective.

Chief executive officers and business owners can achieve their goals by maximizing their understanding, control, and use of the professionals who work for them and really represent them.

In addition, these professionals—principally the accountants and auditors, both internal and external—should work together as a combined force to protect the company's assets and enhance its efficiency.

Finally, learning from the vast experience of auditors and analysts, there are special administrative practices that can benefit all managers—and auditors looking for useful ways to assess the operations of these managers. Above all else, I stress the need for supportive and positive managerial attitudes as the secret of corporate success.

To sum up this section, I offer the following checklist of the challenges facing today's CEO in the management of the audit network, along with a graphic illustration of the forces surrounding the executive office.

THE SWIRLING CURRENTS: A CHECKLIST

1. The piecemeal and disparate approach to organizational internal control, and the accurate reporting by auditors as to the reliability of these controls, is outmoded and unnecessarily costly.

2. It has fostered enormous economic (and criminal) abuses and is eroding public confidence in the accounting profession, both the accountants who keep the books and the accountants who audit the statements and supporting records.

3. The whole area involves many players and pressure points. Management must assume a more complete role in order to harness the swirling currents more forcefully than in the past. Moving out from the center requires impetus from the center itself (best represented by the right attitude from the CEO) and proper directional pushes from the numerous participants:

Independent external auditors
Internal auditors
AICPA
IIA
Local professional societies
National Assoc. of Accountants
Association of Government Accountants
Municipal Finance Officers Association
Municipal Treasurers Association
GAO
OMB
The host of regulatory agencies
Academic institutions
Investigators
Security forces
Human resources managers
ADP professionals
Special audit groups—state auditors, university auditors, EDP
    auditors
Cost accountants

In Figure 1, this list is depicted as a vortex, with the CEO at
its center.
In Summary:

1. The forces are constantly shifting.
2. Audits must be on line and timely.
3. Top management—often the CEO personally—must direct
   the efforts of the whole network.

INTERNAL/EXTERNAL AUDIT NETWORK—AN OUTLINE

In Part Three, I offer my 22 "Rules of Thumb" to help the CEO
set up and direct the company's audit network to its full advan-

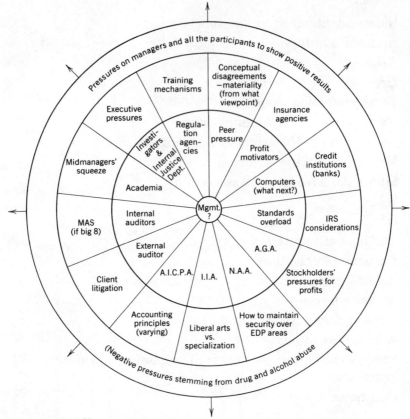

Figure 1. Swirling currents

tage. But, before continuing on to those helpful guidelines, we
provide an outline of the book to this point, showing in concise
form all the issues and components of the audit network, for
quick reader review.

A. Introduction. Concise description of the network and the
   forces at work.
   1. Management is the center point.
      a. Senior executives, operating managers, accounting
         staff, and how they view their responsibilities and re-
         lationships with their internal and external auditors.

    b. Attitude from the center—the cornerstone of reliable internal controls and organizational excellence. Top management sets the accepted patterns so vital for the long haul for ethical and successful enterprises.

2. Independent Internal Auditors: A Part of Management.

    a. Check on internal controls.

    b. Report on the accuracy of records and reports.

    c. Test asset safeguards and the vulnerability of operations.

    d. Look for ways to improve economy and efficiency.

    e. Provide timely, on-line, testing and sampling of data so operating chiefs have a reliable base for making decisions, and so external auditors then can feel reasonably secure in their periodic attest functions.

3. Independent External Auditors: Also a Part of Management.

    a. Contracted by management to assure the public and lenders that books and records are correct and fairly presented.

    b. Sometimes retained by plaintiffs in a legal action, or to comply with laws and regulations, but then they represent different kinds of managers.

    c. Perform other work by special arrangement: systems analysis, special consulting, etc.

4. Professional Societies: Proliferating toward Subspecialties

    a. Set standards, policies, and continuing education requirements.

    b. Operate certification programs.

    c. Work closely with legislative and regulatory bodies, such as SEC, IRS, GAO, etc.

    d. Publish or encourage publication of texts, references, manuals, articles, research papers, and topical pronouncements.

    e. Conduct or sponsor training sessions and seminars.

5. Specialists

    a. Security experts, guards, electronics, physical surveillance, barriers, etc.

    b. Investigative groups, including internal staff as well as the entire law enforcement community.

    c. ADP, sampling, and engineering technicians.

    d. Personnel experts—executive screeners, psychological testers, counselors.

6. Academe

    a. Formal teachers of the network members.

    b. Researchers into new methods; questioners of old methods.

    c. Host for special seminars and extracurricular training.

    d. Oversees and comments intellectually on the whole professional network and its concepts, frequently from a historical perspective.

A. Basic Concerns

1. Internal Controls: The Cornerstone

    a. Wide disagreement, and less than full understanding, of what the network is, how it really functions, and who makes it work.

    b. Administrative functions, accounting processes, separation of duties, vulnerability assessments, self-checking operations—their differences and their similarities.

2. Materiality: Murkiest of all "Common Core" Subjects

    a. What is material changes with the perch of the viewer.

    b. What is material to the external auditor's balance sheet may not be material for considerations of economy in the internal auditor's view. This is an important element.

3. Generally Accepted Accounting Principles: Too Broad for Absorption

    a. Professionals are still writing hundreds of articles each year on the proper handling of: pension costs, inventory pricing, accrual versus cash bases, handling of subsidiaries, contingent liabilities, future predictions, sampling reliability and use, compliance testing (how much), prepaid and deferred items, etc.

   b. Leads to standards overload and inability of practitioners to sort out the vital signs.

4. Computerized Data: Expands all the Concerns

   a. It has changed dramatically the entire theory of organizational vulnerability, and its impact on internal controls should be viewed with great urgency.

   b. The theory of "compartmentalization" to reduce the risk of error, deliberate or inadvertent.

   c. Computer matching—a powerful ally.

   d. Choosing between ADP auditors and traditional auditors who can handle computer operations.

   e. Future of micros in the field.

5. Economy, Efficiency, Effectiveness: How to Consider

   a. The wastefulness of disparate efforts.

   b. Who is the principle cost watcher?

   c. Management's lack of signals to the network.

   d. The danger of doing the wrong thing better and better!

6. Educational Needs and Concerns

   a. More hard-hitting practical and advanced courses with material on modern auditing.

   b. More interchange of ideas between senior and executive practitioners and teachers.

   c. Many of the best courses are being run by in-house or private groups.

   d. Paucity of training budgets. Travel to training sites regarded as a reward or "perk," and not in favor with the public.

   e. Unwillingness by some executives and managers to admit that added practical training is a present need for them and their subordinates.

7. Internal/External Auditor Relationships

   a. Not close enough.

   b. Standards, techniques, education, and capabilities are

all similar, but audit programs often not mutually supportive and reinforcing.

A. The Whole Body Analogy: How to Recognize a Good Working Model
   1. The Concept: How to View It
      a. The well human being does not function as a group of separate, disconnected parts, but a composite of symbiotic and independent cooperative pieces that must work together; so should organizations function for best results.
   2. Organizational Imperatives
      a. The meshing of roles can be very cost effective.
      b. Training and educational functions can be similarly compatible.
      c. Basic checklists of who does what and when. Not fixing responsibility can lead to nobody being responsible for anything.
A. Benefits of a Better Coordinated System
   1. Reduced Management Vulnerability
   2. Lessening the Odds of Legal Actions
   3. Greater Public Assurances that Things Are As Represented
   4. Reduced Opportunities for Ongoing Fraud and Abuse
   5. More Cost Beneficial and Profitable Audits

3

Twenty-two
Rules of Thumb
for
Audit Effectiveness

In Parts 1 and 2, we set out all the parts of the network, and described particular problems faced by the CEO in harnessing the swirling currents to make the network function for the corporate good. The players and their roles were presented, and recommendations made for better management of the whole system.

In the following pages, we offer 22 Rules of Thumb. Those who have read the earlier book in this series, *Audit Logic: A Guide to Successful Audits,* will recognize the format of these "rules" as being very similar to the helpful point sheets in the previous book.

They were designed purposely to give the busy corporate executive or business owner a thumbnail sketch of each important management point involving the audit network. The format allows quick reading and ready reference. Ever cognizant of the demands on the CEO's time, and the unceasing stream of management texts vying for this individual's attention, we offer succinct and helpful guidelines. Implement them, even a portion of them, and we feel confident your audit network will hum along smoothly with minimal intervention needed from "on high."

Many of the rules are not specific to the audit function, but offer advice that can be applied throughout the organization for smoother, more controlled, operations. Further, they can be readily used by all businesses—large and small, profit and non-profit—with equal success.

RULE OF THUMB #1
ON-LINE OPERATIONS

Not Just Important, But Fundamental
Nothing Serves If It Is Not Timely

The potentially powerful combination of external audits and internal audits can be meaningful only if the work follows an orderly plan of timely testing and sampling of the organization data, as they are produced during the fiscal year. Each group's reviews should complement the other. They should be planned in advance of each year's operations. Management has an obligation to set this forth clearly when each year's engagement letter is signed.

Auditing standards repeatedly mention the need for, and the usefulness of, timely testing. One of the most frequently used words in the standards is "timeliness." Being on top of data production and checkouts is critical, for example, in matters involving manufacturing quality control testing, or computer entry of vital data.

We tend to treat computer data and methods of control as matters separate from the rest of the accounting function, but we shouldn't. Computers are essentially fast bookkeepers. Timely scrutiny is needed to keep up with rapid entries, and is critical to controlled and supportable auditing. Clients and the general public are not impressed with audit plans that *intend* to get to certain areas or *will try* to devote resources or allocate coverage to suspected weaknesses.

The whole issue of "stale rolls" is a major component of this timeliness discussion. Putting aside *old* work rather than remaining behind schedule has many merits. (See Rule of Thumb #4, which deals with this as a separate subject.)

Scientific Sampling

As for *scientific sampling* and the on-line process, remember that simply taking a sample of activities at a specific time, or at regular but infrequent intervals, does not tell the tester whether the situation is getting better or worse. The conditions of the operations may be changed, or the recorders of the information may be different; and the infrequent tests may produce unreliable results, especially if the universe if shifting.

Political polling is a good example of how untimely sampling leads one astray. Many voters just don't know how they will vote until they move the lever. Of course, it is impossible to take polls in the booth; but in business, in a sense, it is a possibility. Reliable quality controls absolutely depend on timely testing at every key stage of the production run. Any time there is a material change (see Rule of Thumb #9 on Materiality) in the *people* producing anything, including information, or the *conditions* under which it is produced, or in the *material* itself (perhaps a new supplier, a new run, or a new dye lot), then very careful rechecking (sampling) of the current quality is a must for accuracy and reliability.

Sampling Is the Basis of Testing—Testing Is the Very Foundation of the Whole Audit Process

Sampling. It may be time to reexamine our thinking on this cornerstone to the validation of evidence in the auditing field. I am beginning to believe that we may have let statisticians distort the whole process with some erroneously (and I use the word advisedly) narrow approaches that present only partial pictures, or blurred images, or—worse yet—may even be *mathematically* (!) wrong for audit use.

Modern day sampling probably began with the advent of assembly lines. Management grew concerned that there be no deterioration of work quality creeping into the process, hence the term "quality control." Test techniques had to be scientific, cost-efficient, and timely. How to achieve this?

1. There had to be no deviation of kinds of items produced, no groupings of "almost alike" items. There was to be no guessing that the universe was homogeneous. There was no need for fancy sampling footwork on "clusters," "stratification," "intervals," "multistage," "dollar-unit," and the like, to artificially create homogeneousness.

2. There was no room for any degree of allowable error, of any but the merest defect, in number or extent. No off-the-cuff decisions had to be made as to what represented a good situation, or a bad one, and by how much, in advance or after the fact.

3. The factors of production had to remain constant: same materials, same workers or those with nearly identical work background and experience, same production facility, and the same motivation (initiated by management and carried out by the work force) to produce error-free widgets, or whatever.

4. The sampling, or testing, methods had to be sufficient for extrapolation, and scientifically reproducible—the true test for a laboratory or production line verification.

5. It had to be completely on-line. That is, the procedure(s) completed in a systematic, timely fashion, by the same tester, or testing device, and not performed after the fact.

6. There could be no guesses as to related conditions before, or after, that would affect any so-called confidence levels, nor any reviews of internal systems that purported to present to the sampler a basis for adding or subtracting from the reliability of the universe as represented by the sample itself.

Contrast these six prerequisites with conditions facing the modern-day auditor, or reviewer, in today's intricate, computer dynamic (and consequently very vulnerable), volatile world. Questions arise such as:

Are the standard textbook approaches to audit sampling valid and useful? Are they sufficiently reliable?

Is the audit universe ever really homogeneous? Data production is ever changing with regard to the producers (clerks) and the product. Can one say, for example, that sales slips are ever alike? Certainly the individual attention they get must vary with their quantity, nature, and conditions of sale, and any peculiarities of the sales slip or basic recording mechanism.

Then there are the subtle, but important, motivational factors that can never be considered absolutely stable or constant. These include the relative fatigue of data entry personnel, their awareness of pay differences (the grudge factor), inexperience of the new hire, boredom of routine felt by the old hand, and the relative educational level (those too educated for the job tend to be less accurate than those with fewer extraneous thoughts percolating around). Moreover, the supervisory personnel may feel differently on different days and, through varying levels of supervision, increase or decrease the attention span of the clerks.

The "acceptable" rate of error is in itself a moving target. Its standard depends on the reviewer's judgment, or that of the manager, and what motivation for excellence, coupled with production goals, are currently in force. Who is to say that a 95 percent confidence level (a customary comfort zone) is alright? Doesn't this vary with each distinct business? This "tolerable" deviation rate, or the maximum rate of system failure the auditor can live with and still conclude that the internal controls are operating effectively, is a vague definition at best—and a troublesome process to rely on, at worst.

Suppose the error rate is determined to be high. There still remain some crucial unanswered points. Is the "production line" getting better or worse? Who or what is responsible for the problem and its solution? Which items among the entire universe being studied need fixing, and how do we find them? Are the big-item errors one-time abberances, or, under the present system, always a distinct possibility? Can we scientifically presume that another like sample will produce like results, when the people involved and the underlying systems are always undergoing changes in reliability.

Each sample, drawn from the same period, includes items that were handled differently, by different people, under differing conditions, sometimes quite material. Administrative processes never stand still; and the point is that in many cases there are, essentially, no like samples, ever.

Last, but certainly not the least, of these considerations is the *override principle,* which recognizes that all the controls evaporate, all the quality reviews are for naught, and all the projections fall short if top management decides to superimpose its own methods on either the accounting or reporting process.

Assuming all the above to be concerns valid to the crucial sampling environment, what then should the whole sampling process hinge on? What is useful, reliable, and cost beneficial? Why not on-line methods? Back to basics? Back to the original inspection technique for quality assurance, the essence of good sampling, with the following steps:

1. Make each universe that is to be analyzed homogeneous and try to simulate the fundamental process inherent in the old assembly line. Contain it, or partition it into tight little packages, to make the subject of analysis uniform.

2. Establish a tolerable rate of error—by law, by custom, by industry, by internal management, whatever—and adhere to it consistently for both reporting and settlement purposes. Realize that no system can be perfect. A certain error level should be allowed; but it must be consistent, and known in advance. Don't change the rules once the game's begun.

3. Adhere to a program of continuous, on-line testing. It is very difficult, and often misleading, to come in at a later date and try to "reconstruct" a situation or determine the previous financial condition and accounting accuracy for settlement (or appraisal) purposes. Here is where on-site, internal auditors can perform at their very best and assume their most helpful role, with minimum expense. Because they are there every day, their verifications can be timely and at the right intervals for perfect coverage.

4. Avoid reliance on hard-to-gauge internal controls that dictate the basic confidence levels in the sampling methods. Shun skimpy samples that often require the later importation of "experts" for retroactive certification. It may be possible to extrapolate from such short samples, but always presume a clean universe. The bottom line, then, is continuous, on-line testing throughout the audit period for full coverage—old-fashioned quality control!

There are some in the field of statistics who are advancing the concept of "random multipliers." In effect, they say that single happenings, or small "affectors," can frequently multiply events into certain avenues that can be directly traced to the causal event and are not attributable to the accuracy of the "current" process. If this general theory has merit, it surely supports my asking the reader to accept the necessity of current and timely validations; so these small "affectors" that could increase in importance can be spotted and brought to the surface for study and consideration, as they happen. An example: a switch in a key personnel assignment, or a company policy change, that adversely affects certain people. These would certainly have an effect—maybe serious—on quality and performance later.

One additional point to consider is that of the oft-mentioned "bell curve" that symbolizes a normal, predictable distribution of data, or events. In the data bases studied by auditors, the customary curve is rarely found. Rather, it may take any one of the six forms illustrated in Figure 2. It is also important to note that the curve changes from time period to time period as the evidential details are studied.

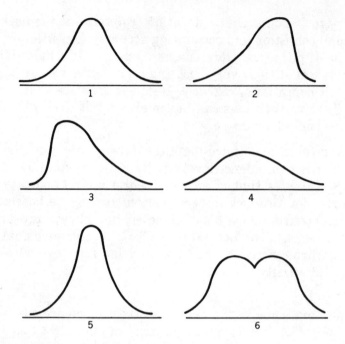

Figure 2.   Six bell curves

Timely Actions Allow Management to Recognize and Reward Performance

Rewards can be formal and substantial, or simple kind words and pats on the back. Recognition can also take the form of well-worded, and timely, criticism. The current abundance of business prose emphasizing organizational excellence makes this point clearly. Performance must be approved or admonished *on the spot* in order to achieve maximum results.

Thirty-nine steps for starting and finishing a timely audit

1. Get a "fix" on the assignment: Is it a balance sheet audit, performance audit, compliance check, internal review, or what?

2. Obtain related material: reports, tax returns, previous work papers.

3. Study industry analyses of related organizations.

4. Set time budgets. Change them later if needed and warranted.

5. Get commitments of adequate staff resources (as prescribed by standards).

6. Hold an entrance conference to set mutual objectives.

7. Have the auditee help with preliminary working data (A/R, A/P reconciliations, prior inventories, ADP equipment and operating data, etc.).

8. Get a senior client commitment for administrative support.

9. Prepare a survey guide to ensure full audit coverage.

10. Physically inspect the entire organization.

11. Relate (mentally) physical characteristics to basic records (people, equipment, etc.).

12. Correlate steps 10 and 11 with organizational and process flow charts. (Keep it simple for a bird's eye understanding.)

13. Set up a series of survey tests to tentatively decide on strong and weak points.

14. Pay strict attention to cash, the most vulnerable of all assets. Be careful, especially if working under ADP processes.

15. Scrutinize other balance sheet and profit and loss items (A/R, A/P, cost of sales, etc.). Analyze them for extremes and material aberrances. (Remember, nothing happens in an organization all by itself.)

16. Scrutinize plant operations for hazards, security, obvious inefficiencies, cleanliness, etc. These are useful clues.

17. Always carefully check internal controls, keeping in mind the very important distinction between administrative controls (urgent) and accounting practices (less vulnerability).

18. Check union arrangements, pension funds, etc.

19. Keep in mind "what could go wrong." An auditor must be able to spot gross misapplications.

20. Know sampling distinctions—acceptance (for surveys), probability (for settlement purposes).

21. Sample only a homogeneous (clean) universe.

22. Decide (before sampling) why something is being tested.

23. Decide what would be an error (before sampling).

24. Determine how the sample will be used.

25. Be able to scientifically distinguish between probability and judgment samples.

26. Study averages and what they mean (or purport to mean).

27. Understand dispersion and distribution concepts.

28. Use the strength of the computer itself to pry open key aberrances from auditee's computer data through the technique of computer matches (a form of "komputer karate"—See Rule of Thumb #10 for a complete discussion of this subject).

29. Insist on extensive staff training in sampling and computer operations.

30. Do not leave computer auditing to "computer wizards" who don't know audit logic.

31. Check computer security—look for "compartmentalization," the separation of *physical* and administrative processes.

32. Match computer results to other material disclosed in the full audit processes.

33. Don't be overwhelmed by cost accounting auditing and conceptualization. Extensive prestudy is inefficient; each case is different.

34. Stay alert to fraud—the ugly specter. It takes many forms and is of great concern to management and to auditors.

35. Sharpen your reporting skills. Reports are the real end product of an audit. Clearly written reports won't mislead the reader in any way.

36. Aim recommendations correctly. Describe who takes corrective action and how.
37. For staff findings at all levels, abide by the old adage: no surprises.
38. Get responsive replies. Make sure they are clear and determine whether there are concurrences or not.
39. Have a frank exit conference, necessary insurance for auditee and auditor.

Source: Extracted with permission from AUDIT LOGIC: A Guide to Successful Audits by Philip Kropatkin. New York: John Wiley & Sons, 1984.

Audit Technique. An Output-First Mentality Can Be Applied Successfully to Many Specific and Practical Verification Methods Found in the Auditor's Portfolio

For example, in the important area of payroll, a high expense item, quite material and certainly sensitive, how should auditors test the accuracy of the organization's pay system in a quick and timely fashion?

The best and most logical way to start is to test the *output*. Select one or more homogeneous work-force areas and judge the accuracy of the actual paychecks by tracing the payment all the way back to the personnel authorizations and related policies or regulations. The results will dictate the next step. If they are sufficiently accurate (and what would be deemed "sufficient" is, of course, another related audit decision), the auditor can proceed to the next question.

Was the accounting system that produced the paycheck procedurally stable and efficient? The underlying point is that the opinion regarding the accuracy and reliability of the paycheck (output) is the determinant that triggers off the needed audit "logic." Often we find that ADP auditors would first study the full ADP system and internal payroll system controls. This is an unnecessarily costly and involved process.

Study and test the sample (output) first. If (and this is an important "if"), there is a high error rate, then look for the systemic cause. It may not actually be the system at all, but merely one or more careless payroll clerks gumming up the works.

RULE OF THUMB #2
ACCEPTED PATTERNS

The Real Key to the Inner Personality of an Organization

People working within an organization, and those called in from the outside, must understand the organizational attitudes and behavior patterns that have a direct bearing on how they do their jobs. How these attitudes and patterns affect the reliability of data and operations should be keenly understood by those responsible for checking their accuracy—the auditors.

The CEO Sets the Accepted Patterns of Behavior

Much like children adopt the patterns of behavior of their parents, so do workers in an organization learn behavior from the managers. When cheating or "fudging" at the executive level becomes apparent to subordinates, it sets an accepted pattern throughout the organization. Some CEOs feel the end justifies the means, any means. They just *want* results and let their managers know they won't look too closely at *how* those managers achieve them. This sets the stage for fraud and abuse. To survive inside this type of organization, the player must follow the unwritten, but potent rules.

If auditors don't have the savvy to spot this attitude in the businesses they audit, they run the certain risk of missing material misapplications—one of the cardinal sins of noncompliance with standards.

Conversely, there are organizations where the CEO, through word and deed, exemplifies a system of values that leads to more positive accepted patterns, and, accordingly, to high quality, profitable production.

Organizations Must Tolerate Some Failed Attempts

Attempts at innovation occasionally don't succeed. They shouldn't be discouraged. If you chew out an earnest manager for a miscue, don't expect that individual to be productive and innovative immediately thereafter. It won't happen.

Too Much Information Can Be Bad for Business

Too often today we find hard-driving CEOs riding their managers for reports, data, and more reports. In some cases, the members of their management teams are spending literally half their work hours producing reams of data in preparation for the monthly three-day "retreat," where they will then pour over it all.

That managers then must spend most of their nights and weekends getting their regular work done is a negative side effect of the information age. Just because we have the capability to generate endless information doesn't mean we necessarily need it all. Not only can it lead to "analysis paralysis," where no action is taken, just more and more information generated, but it can destroy the health and vitality of the organization through top-level executive "burnout." When burnout leads to "bail out," the time and expense of recruiting others and getting them up to speed, only to repeat the cycle, drains the organization's energy.

Those CEOs who would point to corporate profits as justification for such patterns should first be sure that a different approach would not have earned even more. If this is an accepted pattern in your organization, identify it—and eliminate it.

Don't Treat the Audit Effort as Small Stuff

An accepted pattern very important to internal auditors is the way the CEO handles audit findings and recommendations. If these are treated perfunctorily and relegated to lower-level action committees or, worse yet, left entirely in the hands of the audited department's manager to comply with, then the executive messages are quite clear: They don't think much of the audit effort in general or of the value of the audit chief as a consultant. The organization will know and respond accordingly.

Serious executive-level consideration of the findings, and action on recommendations, will communicate the importance of the audit function. This accepted pattern will allow it to perform well.

Corporate Attitudes: A Sports Analogy

How many times have we seen baseball or football team owners, dissatisfied with their teams' most recent results, up and fire the manager? They bring in a new manager to "shake up" the team—one with a reputation for being hardnosed, or one with "quick fix" hire and fire authority. What is deceptive here is that positive results are often very short-lived. And it often takes years, and considerable expense, to rebuild what these people "fixed."

Contrast this situation with truly effective teams, or sports dynasties, that have produced winners (and gate revenues) over the long haul: the Celtics, the Cowboys, the good 'ol Yankees. They evidenced consistent, solid managerial skills that discouraged destructive "hot-dogging" in favor of respected team play.

Modern management can learn a great deal from the perceptive patterns and methods of big-time sports organizations that consistently produce winners. There are few mysteries or secrets in their techniques.

RULE OF THUMB #3
THE OVERRIDE PRINCIPLE

Internal Controls Evaporate When Top Management Overrides Them

No system of accounting processes, or administrative techniques, or control, can defend itself against continued undermining by management. It is the correct attitude of the CEO that leads to real control, not going through the motions of checking for appearance's sake.

The Essence of Sound, Workable, Top-Down Internal Control

The controls become super potent if management consistently pursues them with apparent honesty and continuity, and with regular communication to the staff. Staff members need to know the CEO will enforce the rules, not just give lip service.

Internal checklists are useful, but only really effective if the CEO strenuously insists they are "checked off"—again, not just there for window dressing.

A question I am often asked at seminars, usually by a city treasurer or clerk, is: "What should I do if the mayor asks me to pay for items that are unauthorized or are over the appropriation limit established by the city council?" I answer with a new question: "How material is the request?" If it is a trivial sum, then my answer is, "Forget it." (If this is but an isolated case.) But, if it represents a pattern of abuse of procedures and may be for material sums, the situation then becomes serious. This is the override principle at work.

Even more difficult to handle is the CEO's asking the controller to issue checks for a separate fund that only the CEO has knowledge of and access to. More override. What then? Each case deserves individual consideration *and* action.

In the numerous and widely publicized incidences of corporate fraud in recent years, a common denominator in most cases has been that the audit techniques were consistently sound throughout, both by internal auditors and external CPAs. Behind the scenes, either management "cooked" the books or overrode the established mechanisms for process control. What also became known in most cases is that the auditors had their suspicions—or outright knowledge—that the existing controls were being either ignored or bypassed. Private ledgers, and/or a management attitude that eschewed established procedures, were discovered.

Investigative Clues

Among other things, items like unorthodox travel reimbursement, and free merchandise, often "tip off" the auditors, either in or out of the company, to investigate additional, more meaningful fraud on other levels.

Where Were the Auditors?

The recent disclosures regarding the plight of the Ohio Savings Banks, and a considerable number of municipalities around the country, have prompted many individuals to ask: Why aren't seriously weak links in a financial system, or deficiencies in important operations of any organization, brought to light by the auditors . . . before they get out of hand? The answer, disconcertingly, involves more questions. Both in this particular case, and as a general hypothesis.

First . . . in this instance, just what auditors are we talking about? The savings institutions and municipalities that were harmed in this particular defalcation by the investment group utilized by these organizations were probably too small to have an internal audit staff of their own. The investment firm, even if it did have its own internal auditors (and it is not clear yet whether they did or did not), surely would not have permitted any in-house auditors to make any significant inroads into their inner secrets. The point—when the chief officers of a firm are directly involved in questionable practices, the normal rules of what workload the internal auditor schedules, or does not schedule, are not operable. Audit independence is restricted. *Internal controls are seriously threatened, if not totally destroyed, when the managing officers of an organization decide to override them for personal gain,* whether they just be contrary to corporate policy or for outright illegal purposes.

What about the bank or municipality's external auditors? . . . Here is where an entirely different set of forces come into play. For one thing the external auditor does not normally have an on-line resident force in place in the subject organization. He has as a main objective the "snapshot" requirement for Balance Sheet and P&L attestation at year-end. He would normally be expected to independently verify the actual ownership and existence of the government securities that were supposedly backing up the repurchase agreements. But if this were not perceptively done with the third party holding banks, and were only verified with the faulty investment firm, then the auditor would not necessarily be alerted to the potential impropriety. As for the external auditors of the investment firm that has jeopardized the clients they serviced, there are reports that a partner in the auditing firm engaged to attest to the statements is being charged by the SEC for civil fraud. What can protect the public against this type of situation? One more factor comes to mind. The public itself did not serve as a general "scrutinizing" agent sitting in the wings, as they might do with publicly held corporations they invest in. Banks and municipalities are assumed to be less in the need of close scrutiny than are highly competitive, or possibly under-capitalized for-profit organizations.

If there is an overriding theme that should emerge from the disclosures of the Ohio affair—and so many like it, but without the same widespread notoriety, . . . it is this: Our business world has to look to "management" for the hard answers to the need for true internal controls! Management should harness the potent audit forces at its command and make the entire "Internal/External Audit Network" the combinative team that it was conceptually meant to be.

Modern business complexities have made the piecemeal and disparate approach to organizational internal control, and accurate reporting by all auditors as to how reliable these controls are, outmoded and unnecessarily costly. The Ohio affair is obviously a good case in point. It has fostered enormous economic (and criminal) abuses and is eroding public confidence in the accounting profession . . . both the accountants who keep the books, and the accountants who audit the reported statements and underlying records.

The whole subject has so many players and pressure points to deal with, and from every conceivable direction, that it becomes clearer all the time that the focal point at the center of this "vector of forces"—management—must assume its full role in order to harness the "swirling currents" and move the center. But this requires concerned impetus by the center itself (the right attitude on the part of the corporate executives) as well as proper directional pushes from the various and exceedingly widespread participants. Some of these are: independent external and internal auditors. AICPA, IIA, NAA, AGA, MFOAB, MTA (and all their local branches). GAO, OMB (with all the regulatory agencies), academic institutions, prosecutory, security and investigative forces, personnel and EDP specialists . . . the list could continue.

What is also a problem is that the various forces can be: aligned in one direction, diametrically opposed, partially pointed the same way, or what is additionally frustrating, shifting from time to time, depending on inner organizational thrusts. All this which can be seen reflected in current high level discussions about the true meaning of "materiality" (it seems to change with the of the viewer) and what internal really means, which brings up this critical point. Unless an audit or review function is on-line—that is timely—it may be, and probably is, weak! All the standards emphasize this point. This is where management can infect a powerful directional push . . . by insisting that its audit internal and external, work together to best advantage. Considering the potential explosiveness of the current computer scene, timeliness of the examination functions is one of the most important deterrents to keeping errors, inadvertant or otherwise, from festering and becoming more material than they need to be.

In summary, the whole network can be better put together for positive good, and more public protection, by the managerial forces at the center of each discreet business matrix. The Ohio case surely is a case in point. One cannot expect the auditors to provide the vital push, more or less alone. The first question, when trouble erupts, should more accurately be . . . *where was management?*

Source: *Auditalk,* Institute of Internal Auditors, April 1985.

RULE OF THUMB #4
THE STALE ROLLS SYNDROME

Put Aside Old Items; Stay Current—A Small Price to Pay for Bigger Returns Essential for On-Line Control

Throw away the leftover breakfast rolls! Don't add them to the next day's fresh rolls and eat them first, with the fresh rolls becoming tomorrow's leftovers. You end up eating stale rolls forever. The cost of becoming current is only the price of a few rolls.

If the staff cannot reconcile or handle one day's items, have them put these aside so that the next day's work remains current. Don't stack up unfinished material continuously, so that nothing is ever timely. The insidiousness of this is devastating to good control, anywhere in the operations. Untimely internal audits are practically worthless, making the external audits that depend on them unreliable or unworkable. Very costly!

Two—of Many—Detrimental Side-Effects of Stale Rolls

1. When managers and supervisors fall behind in reviewing the work of subordinates, they often fail to get out in the field at important review times. Then they are reduced to reliance

upon after-the-fact paper reviewers rather than the more effective on-the-job senior planners and control executives.

2. Checking and running over stale material causes key people to lose the opportunity to review new ideas in a timely fashion and come up with innovative material. They are always cleaning up old work. By the time they clear up the backlog, there is a new load on its way, putting them right back where they started—handling outdated transactions.

One can see evidence of the stale rolls syndrome in everyday life. Many states, for example, require cars to be tested periodically to assure they are safe to operate and meet environmental standards for emissions. Using this to illustrate my point, contrast what happens in two different states:

State 1

You take your safety test and pass. After a brief (20 to 30 minute) wait, you pick up your new laminated driver's license. You—as a driver—and your car—as a vehicle driven on public roads—are designated "safe."

State 2

Not so, here. Although the test in this state is just as quick, license renewal is not. You receive a temporary license with the explanation that you will receive your permanent license through the mail in about six weeks.

Why so long? Somewhere along the way, State #2's motor vehicle office let its operations become stale, and never caught up. Six weeks has become the norm for license renewal—a permanently untimely process. It takes only a few minutes for each separate license renewal to be handled, but it is almost six weeks before each one receives attention. It would most likely be simple—and cost beneficial—to augment the system with more people, or strip it of red tape, to get current. It would also lead to safer roads and drivers.

I have found such everyday examples to be remarkably similar to the processes at many plants and business offices. Some are forever handling old items, sometimes even speeding up and slowing down as a matter of course because they are accustomed to a certain backlog!

An Example of Stale Rolls in Business—Audit Periods to Be Covered

Auditors seem to feel compelled when they start a new audit to go back automatically to the last time the particular area was audited and start their detailed checking and sampling of evidence from that period forward to the present. This is not necessary and usually constitutes a gross waste of time. Who needs or can use information that pertains to an outdated period? The conditions have changed, the people are different, the old is no longer pertinent. The auditors should examine *current* transactions—right up to the present time if they want to be useful (*and heard*).

The auditors' belief that they must provide a continuous and uninterrupted picture of the area under scrutiny is false. For example: Auditors, in determining their annual work plan, or targets of opportunity, can choose between whole functions or programs within those functions. Then why can they not similarly choose among periods, and stay with current (and useful) material, omitting old data? *They can.*

If auditors, both internal and external, cannot momentarily don the thinking caps of management, both with respect to the big picture of the business, and to the tasks at hand that day, and tune into the needs of the CEOs they serve, then they merely go through the motions of a routine—perhaps meaningless—review in routine compliance with standards. Rather, they must be timely in their studies and timely in their recommendations.

RULE OF THUMB #5
BOTTLENECKS

It Takes the Quick Action of the CEO to Open Up the Bottleneck and Release the Flow

Depending on subordinate managers to handle this task may not be wise. CEOs should be ever alert to situations where they may be needed to step in and authorize action to smooth the way. Even small, isolated bottlenecks can harm an organization.

One Short Example

A purchasing department, in accordance with department policies, has exhausted itself in local searches for an urgently needed spare part, to no avail. The CEO—and perhaps the CEO alone—has the authority to say: "Get on a plane to Los Angeles, buy the part, and get right back."

Bottlenecks Obstruct Efficient Management

Although hard to classify, you know them when you see them, if you stay attuned to their nature and significance. When management is *aware* of a major operational bottleneck, it usually can marshall its forces and overcome the impediment.

Very often, it is the smaller things that fall outside of normal supervisory circles and perhaps loom as too "routine" for top attention that internal auditors can spot and point out, often to great advantage.

Example 1: Servicing Customers Waiting in Lines

This is an everyday business problem—at banks, ticket windows, airline counters, supermarket checkouts. When complications with one customer (a complaint, a credit card approval, an enormous basketful) hold up the whole process inordinately, the bottleneck can be removed by an adroit manager or supervisor who opens a new counter or takes the "special" customers out of the line to handle separately.

Example 2: The Reproduction Facility (Copy Room) that is Centralized in an Attempt at Efficiency

I have yet to meet an executive who believes this to be an improvement over copy machines sprinkled judiciously about, yet the facilities managers will have their way. When one manager needs something fast, an assistant waits on line, often behind others with stacks of copying. Where is the efficiency? The originator waits, the clerk or assistant wastes time—all in the name of economy (false economy in this case).

What frequently follows this bottleneck is department heads acquire their own copy machines and "bootleg" their use—not an economical move in terms of quantity purchase discounts, and so forth. Centralized copying should be for major, time-flexible documents. Localized copiers, with log-in sheets to reduce employee theft, make more sense.

Example 3: The Telephone

This superb instrument, an integral part of our everyday personal and business life, can, if an organization is not watchful, become a bottleneck in itself. Three ways come to mind:

Managers tend to give telephone interruptions priority over personal visits. Conversations hang in mid-sentence while the supervisor or manager handles the call in the visitor's presence. Often, other calls follow in quick succession. If those kept waiting are at a disadvantage—someone there for a job interview, or a sales call, for example—they will, of course, wait; but another company employee trying to accomplish a day's tasks may leave to try again another time. Wasteful. Hold calls during scheduled meetings.

Another telephone bottleneck occurs when callers from the outside can't get past a mechanical message telling them they are in line for a real person to become available to take their calls. How frustrating, especially if they sought only a simple answer to a simple question, or confirmation of an upcoming appointment. How negative to cash flow if they wanted to place an order, but in frustration and disgust called another supplier instead. Such systems should have built-in controls that tell how many calls were lost.

The third telephone bottleneck occurs when a department head or supervisor doesn't take measures to assure that emergency calls from senior-level executives are routed right through to them when they are elsewhere in the plant or offices. Often, time is of the essence; and frequently the senior executive will go to someone else for the answer, perhaps getting only the second-best insight.

Service organizations, such as hospitals and health maintenance organizations, whose speedy response can mean life itself, must keep their telephone call receiving system in flawless working order. Sales organizations, too, can and should regard incoming telephone lines as their life's blood; and, if they pay for toll-free incoming lines, make sure those calls are answered promptly and the callers not left on hold.

An Audit Story of CEO Bottleneck Bashing

Sometimes it takes a bold (but often simple and inexpensive) executive step to sweep aside silly bottlenecks. Some years back, a colleague and I were assigned to a closing audit at a bustling steel fabricating plant in Tennessee. When we arrived, the comptroller (a customary working host in these situations) informed us that working space was very tight and asked us to accommodate ourselves in what might kindly be called a substandard office. To be polite, we agreed.

When the president of the company came by later to say hello, he was furious at the situation and quickly responded by sending two clerks home for a few days, with pay, to free up their office for our use. He said our important work for the company took precedence. Of course he was right. This story typifies how oftentimes only upper management can see the big picture.

All employees should know they have an obligation to help

remove bottlenecks wherever they see them. Suggestions should be rewarded whenever possible—even if only verbally.

Establish Organizational Priorities

Bottlenecks are frequently tied in to the stale rolls syndrome, in that supervisors will take all their review assignments in absolute order, finishing them one by one, neither raising distress signals when overloaded nor sorting the super-important from the less crucial.

The Most Insidious Organizational Bottleneck— Managerial Stubbornness

A refusal by management to face up to a set of facts that just can't be handled in a normally acceptable way often requires the most sophisticated approach to overcome.

The Sea Captains' Split

Another audit story, as an example of this stubbornness and how to handle it, concerns three partners who owned four ships. For a variety of reasons, they decided to split up and go their separate ways. This was not an adversarial situation. I represented the partner of a CPA firm whose client was one of the trio. My assignment was to familiarize myself with the ship charter business and to know these particular freighters so well as to be able to suggest the split most advantageous to our client. This, I quickly ascertained, would be a nearly impossible task.

Consider these facts: Each ship, although of the same general class and size, had different equipment (an extra anchor, added radar devices, a new coat of paint). Each was operating under varying charter rates depending on its last contract; all had crews different in size and character, therefore differing labor costs. There was a variety of tax backgrounds (each ship was under a separate corporate structure). They were in port and under sail, and each was running up expenses every minute under the absolute control of its own skipper. There were varying dates as to when they last underwent Coast Guard inspection—a potentially high expense could be in the offing for repairs. Contingent taxes were different. The book-keeping for the four vessels in effect never, never caught up with the situation. Ticker tapes recorded expenses as they occurred on the high seas—but it was continuously and unpredictably changing.

The point to all this: There was no way to get a fix on what each vessel was actually worth at any one specific moment with any degree of accuracy. The value of each vessel was going up and down all the time, but in relative terms, they were close in value. What to do. My superior kept pressing me for more and more details, and I went back and forth working them out. I told him early on that this situation was not applicable to "normal" or usual accounting determinations and should be approached in a different manner. I suggested one day that the partners take the three of the vessels closest in value and, figuratively, put them in a hat. Each partner, on a given "closing" date, would draw one vessel. The fourth would be sold to the highest outside bidder as of that date, and the cash proceeds from this sale split three ways.

My suggestion was summarily dismissed with this decree: "High powered accounting firms can always determine the true net worth of anything as of any cut-off date." I was sent back for more and more current information, which was in .effect shifting under my very nose more quickly than I could create new analyses and summarize them.

To make progress, we had to reexamine the base, stop being stubborn, and remove the mental "bottleneck" impeding an innovative and practical approach to a unique business and accounting conundrum.

Thankfully, the three partners, being experienced and practical businessmen, finally adopted my suggestion and parted ways on this joint venture, completely satisfied. But what a waste of expensive talent. Each partner's accountants had spent a lot of time doing exactly what I worked to avoid once my initial survey indicated the path of least resistance.

And, checking back later, the other accountants also sensed that the best course was to make a quick, sensible split based on the owners' insights.

The Point!

The CEOs (in this case, the three partners) should have taken charge of their network of professionals and made them listen to what the practicalities were and what should be done—not the other way around. This is the very essence of good networking.

RULE OF THUMB #6
THE NORUMBEGA PRINCIPLE
(Let's Not Always Accept the Generally Accepted)

Background

Years ago—in the sixteenth and seventeenth centuries—someone started drawing maps of the area off the New England coastline, erroneously identifying part of it as "Norumbega," probably based on some early voyages, and some romantic notions. For many years, cartographers identified this area on their maps. Some limited it to a smaller area; others enlarged it to include the whole coast from Cape Breton to Florida. Most historians now agree it never existed. But, if you were to pick up *Webster's International Dictionary*, 2d edition, published in 1959, and look up "Norumbega," you would assume by its definition it did indeed exist:

"A region along the NE coast of N. America, or its capital city, given on old maps. The extent of the country varied widely."

The Norumbega Principle

"The citing and perpetuating of erroneous or irrelevant material, data, and concepts."

Moral: Reexamine the base often.

In the seventeenth century, when ocean travel to America was rare, it was natural to find a dearth of good maps of the New England coastline. The captain of each visiting schooner, however, tried to contribute to the general body of cartographical knowledge of usable ports and inlets for the common good of each succeeding ship.

It was in this fashion that an area known as Norumbega was first charted off the coast of what is now Connecticut, and was shown in the coastal maps of that time and detailed in seafaring literature for the next hundred years.

One early mapmaker probably drew upon some Indian legend and sketched out this detail. Interestingly, subsequent mapmakers merely picked up the earlier drawings without ever verifying they were correct. Researchers are still at a loss to know how it all began.

What Is the Norumbega Scene in Your Organization?

So it goes in many organizations with regard to their data bases, their specific understanding of just what is important to top management, their expectations of how much quality they will forego for quantity production quotas, what cost is tolerable in record keeping, and who will have the information needed to evaluate all these policy questions. All too frequently, the dictates of each system's creators are merely accepted and embellished.

Further, no line of communication between management and the work force is established that would help eliminate the Norumbegas. Modern businesses require such communication to survive in the present competitive market.

Chief executive officers must guard against the Norumbega Principle. The information on which decisions are based must remain forever suspect.

Even the Simplest Statement Must Be Verified

Example: For many years it was assumed that fertile, varied terrains like rain forests were the spawning ground of new forms of life. Not necessarily true, say the "anti-Norumbegaists." Possibly the harsher climates around the poles, the small, isolated communities, spawn the spectacular new animals because the demanding conditions provided the stress needed for any dramatic evolutionary leaps forward. Evidence that the old assumptions can, and should, deserve new perspectives.

Example: In the track and field high jump event, it was always assumed that to jump over the bars, you had to get one leg up over the bar, then propel your body around the top and over. That is, until the "Fosdick" era when it was shown to be better to propel your head over first, then twist backwards before pushing the rest of your body over. Now, once again, some of the best jumpers are returning to the old method with good results. It only shows the need to reexamine the base, regularly.

On the Darker Side

Consider the current real concerns over the use of false identification. Across the country certain documents are taken for granted as authentic identifiers: Social Security cards, drivers' licenses, and credit cards, particularly if someone presents all three. But the simple fact is, once someone counterfeits a "breeder" document, such as a birth or baptism certificate, it is easy to obtain the other accepted forms of identification. All are issued on the strength of the forged "Norumbega" document.

RULE OF THUMB #7
BE ON THE LOOKOUT FOR GIFTED PERFORMERS
WORKING FOR AVERAGE CHIEFS

This Problem is Omnipresent, Yet Often Overlooked by Management

There is not much that will impair an organization more than having a considerable cadre of "so-so" performers trying to manage of staff of better-than-average young comers.

The Problems Can Be Extreme

Innovation grinds to a halt. The most gifted somehow appear otherwise to the mediocre. Creative thinkers, professionals on the cutting edge of their speciality, find it hard to bow easily to musty old management approaches. Either the bright ones leave on their own, or are helped on their way by stodgy supervisors who consider them a threat.

The Management Challenge

To exploit top thinkers and maverick performers by giving them enough freedom to shine, yet keeping them in check just enough to avoid getting the organization into trouble—that is, sufficiently free to move into uncharted areas for real gains to the organization. Particularly in the area of computer technology, there are real gains to be registered, or losses to be suffered. The outcome depends on how the challenge is met.

One Good Solution

Find a sensible yet flexible manager to handle the freewheelers on special assignments. Put the brain cells to work for the good of the organization.

Important Corollary to the Whole Subject of Superthinkers vs. Ordinary Minds

Things and ideas may seem less than top-notch, or extraordinary, if stated in very basic, unembellished terms. The average manager may fail to recognize real expertise and solid knowledge (even genius) if its owner makes instant sense and describes the idea in very simple language.

Two Historical Illustrations

1. Abraham Lincoln was a master at interpreting a political opponent's points of view, and often far better at expressing them than his adversary was. His opponents deeply disliked him for this gift. If any of them had been his boss, his ideas—his brilliance—might have been muffled, or extinguished.

2. When Sir Isaac Newton reported on his theory of gravity— after years of deep thought and study—he was greeted with a "ho hum" response, triggered, most likely, by his simple, clear explanation of the concept.

People who really know what they are talking about can explain their subject to a high school student. But, disconcertingly, they rarely seem ingenious to the average mind. Newton was so offended, he practically went into seclusion for a number of years. This, too, can happen to a gifted employee whose brain waves are received only by dull managers. Often, they strike out on their own, leaving behind a void, and potentially creating strong future competition for their former employer.

Native intelligence can be a great natural resource. Use it. If the road to top management in your company is a circuitous one, travelled only by those who can "endure," reevaluate! Are you keeping bright people in lower-level positions out of a sense of order? If so, to whose benefit?

The "Hot Shot" Shake-up

On the other hand, do not overlook the responsibility of the gifted performer to make every attempt to get along with the designated manager. It is not a one-way street. Hot shots, no matter how special, cannot run roughshod over others. Another balancing act that requires the CEO's insights.

Pick the Right Enemy

I illustrate this Rule of Thumb with personal experience. After basic training in the Army during World War II, I was one of a group of recruits with college experience and a high I.Q. to be sent back to college for special training.

This program lasted for the better part of one year, then was abandoned to meet the increased need for infantry and other combat troops. Along with 30 or 40 others from the program, I joined an infantry company. None of the sergeants in charge was college educated, but all were very earnest and hard-working. By and large, they had our respect; but they couldn't resist "laying it on" us "college types." It didn't work. We were all as strong physically as the non-coms. Anything they could do we could do. The friction was becoming unbearable, until one day several of us called the non-coms together and asked them to lay off. There was no point to it; we vowed to accept their leadership if they would recognize we were not there to show them up, but to get a job done. It worked, because both groups realized the need to work together to defeat a common enemy.

In a corporate vein, this experience applies to health and survival. All benefit from the managers—somehow, the best way they can—getting the job done well, even if it means letting gifted subordinates "do their thing."

Network Considerations

As far as the audit network is concerned, there are a lot of managerial stars out there who do not get involved in the routine tasks of the professionals (principally accountants) under their jurisdiction. The gifted managers leave what they think are fairly routine matters in recording and issuing statements to their technicians without digging in to "help."

Staff vs. Line Considerations

Another angle of this discussion is where managers have both staff and line personnel under their direction. Top-level executives must make it clear to their staff people that they can only function well and with any degree of authority if they are expert at what they do and are right in their recommendations to the CEO. They must be sufficiently "gifted" to function without the formal authority that line officers possess. Here, too, auditors should be especially alert to the pitfalls in this inherently volatile situation.

Open Lines of Communication

Average managers may throw up obstacles, between the rising stars in their command and the CEO, to prevent bright ideas from filtering up. Internal auditors can spot these situations and bring them to the attention of the right executive, thus opening up lines of communication.

An auditor working inside any department should stay attuned to the wavelengths therein, because people will often discuss their frustrations with an outsider willing to listen.

Or, the auditor could make it a point to ask talented people how they would have solved an organizational problem in their domain. This is their opportunity to open up and say they had a great idea long ago which their manager stifled, or suggestions that were ignored.

Gifted people will surely leave if they cannot be recognized; or, worse yet, they will stay and create a "get-even" force that undermines from within. Again, auditors can act as a relief valve for such a force, when engaged in their detailed interviews and investigations, by spotting the "good ideas people" and referring them and their ideas to a higher level for consideration. Management can get valuable leads on who has what in the brains department from the perceptions of impartial internal auditors. What better role for an internal auditor?

RULE OF THUMB #8
BEWARE THE EXECUTIVE "CAMOUFLEUR"

For Business to Work, Information Must Get from One Rung on the Ladder to the Next, Usually via Progress Reports

This rule of thumb acknowledges one potent point: There are always managers who will muddy up production data and camouflage substandard manufactured products to protect themselves. Sometimes the cover-up is of a very minor inaccuracy. On other occasions, it takes on greater proportions. Auditors and accountants must look for the material alteration of facts by camoufleurs in their attempts to hide their misdeeds.

What most often triggers the lies and deception is the culprit's inability to cope with the requirements of the assignment. Sometimes the assignment is unrealistic; other times the manager is misplaced. An almost sure clue: a muddied-up inventory and no programmed on-line audit work by the audit staff in what should be a first-line workload area.

RULE OF THUMB #9
MATERIALITY DEPENDS ON THE PERCH OF THE VIEWER

Conceptually, this entire area has been likened to "Chinese baseball," where the field dimensions and the bases themselves can be changed after the ball is pitched or hit. Applying this to organizational behavior, it is crucial that management communicate to its team what is urgent and vital *before the play starts*—unless it is prepared to play a game of Chinese baseball.

The Concept of Size

Materiality is a philosophy of life, not an accounting principle. Things are only big when "bigger" than other things. Of course, there are some things which are just not comparable to anything: "Life is very peculiar," said the Fly. "Compared to what?" said the Spider, as he ate him for lunch.

One of the best illustrations with respect to the comparison of things was a film I observed at the Air and Space Museum of the Smithsonian Institution in Washington, D.C. The excellent film was produced to illustrate the concept of size and the relative differences of objects.

The film opened with a shot of a man sitting in a beach chair on his back lawn in a seaside suburb or Miami Beach. It appeared to be a normal situation, in a normal setting, deliberately so, to create a starting place.

Then the scene started to shift. The camera moved up and away—from the height of a helicopter to the altitude of a jet—from which perspective the man was very, very small; and the backyard became a mere speck on the Florida coastline. Then, as the camera went even higher, presumably located on a spacecraft, the entire coastline faded away. The next view showed all of North America to be as small as the original man's backyard. The "perch" changed, and the size of the object changed accordingly, at least as it was perceived. What was material to the helicopter pilot was insignificant to the astronaut.

To reverse the illustration, the cameras returned to the person in the backyard and proceeded then to show that this "speck" was enormous when compared to the size of an individual cell in his body; those cells gigantic compared to their molecules, and so on. So "big" and "small" depend on your vantage point, with regard to both size and materiality.

Materiality as Considered from the Differing Perches of the External and Internal Auditors

An excellent example of how internal and external auditors can take differing views of materiality can be found in the considerations shown the important asset of inventories, a major line item on financial statements.

External auditors are mostly concerned with its fair presentation on the financial statements. Their concerns as to materiality in this area center on "putting a dollar value" on the inventory by such means as determining:

Its original cost to the auditee, or
Its market value at the time of audit

If the inventory was manufactured by the company, then its cost in terms of labor, overhead, and materials would be determined. If some of the inventory was only partially finished, then a fair value would be assigned to such work in process. In the course of their examination, external auditors would take appropriate samples and add up the totals.

This would often be done once at year's end. Depending on the overall size of the inventory, they would write off, or disregard, minor errors or differences.

What the External Auditors Don't Find to Be Important, that the Internal Auditors Do

1. Was the merchandise bought or manufactured absolutely first rate and will it satisfy finicky customers? (Consider that this company may have its whole reputation resting on perfect products, for example.)

2. Does this inventory fit in with the company's future sales objectives? The top brass may have decided to change the product line and will have to downgrade the whole inventory.

3. Were there excessive adjustments needed to reconcile the physical counts with the recorded balances (bad procedures)?

4. Were reasonable prices paid for the raw materials, freight, and other charges? Discounts taken?

5. Any undue delays in ordering and receiving raw materials, resulting in slowed production runs?

6. Do ineffective warehouse operations exist? For example, warehousemen cannot locate quickly and accurately what is on hand and therefore may cause faulty shipments or warehouse refusals and unnecessary ordering.

7. Are there proper (or any) controls over "scrap?" (This is a source of real vulnerability, but of minor concern to the external auditors as its overall total may be only a fraction of the regular inventory.)

8. Are there definite safeguards over vulnerable portable items?

9. Are the computer-based day-to-day line item control and reorder practices accurate?

In certifying to the asset value on the balance sheet, the external auditor may not be giving the reader insight as to whether the procedures are getting better or worse regarding the continued reliability of the asset value stated. They may be "materially" changed in short order after the date on the balance sheet because of endemic weaknesses in the system; or, what might be more germane, because the product line is changing due to external conditions, and the inventory is just not as shown on the books, in terms of the ongoing operations.

This is where the internal auditors' reviews can be very important and relevant, and should be embodied in the work of the external auditor to the extent that they are current (on-line) and done in a consistent and independent fashion. Periodic inventorying all during the year with appropriate samples and joint observation can be very productive.

RULE OF THUMB #10
"KOMPUTER KARATE"
(How the Computer Can Be Tamed to Serve)

"Komputer Karate," is a coined phrase meaning that the power of the computer can be harnessed—that one does not need to remain overwhelmed by a profusion of confusing, computer-generated data.

The Problem Can Be Separated into Two Segments

The first is the auditing methods being used and continually improved upon by the auditors in the network. Auditors can and should be a significant part of the management scheme.

The second concerns the analytical vistas opened up by good, large-scale, ADP and how *not* to be held hostage by the masses of available—often dubious—data.

Computerized Accounting and Operational Records Can Be Dealt with Effectively by New Audit Methods that Involve Matching One Set of Records with Another.

Such matching spots anything that auditors have deemed—in advance of the examination—to be at least out of the ordinary. When errors are found, they should be subjected to deeper and extended scrutiny by the audit team. This, in effect, uses the infinite patience and probing ability of the machinery itself to test items that are a part of another machine, so to speak.

All that is needed is existing computerized data and a relatively simply program to "throw out" any items that do not fit a preconsidered point of reference. One must not presume the computer will do the whole job. It will merely take the drudgery out of sorting auditable material and pinpoint all the items that will be subjected to the remainder of the review, steps normally associated with establishing audit credibility.

Other Considerations

Many executives seem to be infatuated with the limitless information potential of computers—sometimes at the real expense of the human thinking that ought to be at the base of any analysis. When playing the enticing "what if" games that computers make available, beware contracting "spreadsheetitis." And remember, machines cannot think (not yet)—they can only rearrange what was furnished them previously.

"Ivory tower" people tend to eschew electronic data from their various divisional directors in favor of in-person reports, with the nuances and ideas that arise from face-to-face encounters.

RULE OF THUMB #11
TRANSOM THEORY

"Just drop the data through the transom—Our accountants will take it from there."

Organizational Information

If relevant and needed, it is real knowledge. All else is costly trivia. The information gatherers are most often the deciders of what is important.

What Data Is Gathered, by Whom, for What Purpose, Must Be Determined by the CEO in Accordance with Company Objectives

The natural question of underlying standards or "norms" now comes into focus. How does an auditor get a clear view of what would constitute a good or bad performance—in advance of any review or examination? When an auditor encounters extremes, at either end of the results spectrum, the reporting of the results is relatively easy. What is terrible is usually very clear and easily reported. Similarly, if the operation looks very good, then there is only the task of explaining the extent (scope) of the review, so the reader will feel confident that the examination was conducted fully and reliably.

When the results are indistinct, or comprise a mixed bag of good and bad, then a summary opinion becomes more difficult. I have asked CEOs how they know their office is "doing a good job," and their replies frequently belied uncertainty.

In profit-making organizations, they can always refer to the bottom line. Did they make a profit? Are the profits increasing each year and are they commensurate with the equity investment, or compatible with industry trends? What they usually cannot answer is whether they have *maximized* their profits. Could they have done better with more control and efficiency?

In nonprofit organizations, or government operations, the answer is much more elusive.

How Audit Logic Can Work

I would like to share experiences that illustrate the point that thinking auditors, with a flair for analytical scrutiny of available statistics, can produce results more illuminating than those produced by traditional analysts.

Example 1: Educational Programs

The department over which I had audit responsibility had created a nationwide educational improvement program targeted at children from educationally deprived families. Grants were awarded to local school districts to emphasize reading and math with these target groups.

Over the Years, the Question Kept Arising: Were These Programs Doing Any Good? Was the Money Well Spent?

We found that educators had been very slow in setting up evaluation systems to determine if the $1 billion spent annually did any good. They wanted years (too slow) of traditional studies to test the results.

What we quickly discovered, however, was that over 20 percent of the money was spent to improve general school facilities and general teaching programs. Obviously, over $200 million each year was incorrectly applied, not specifically directed at the target groups.

Our auditors were not educational "specialists," but the audit logic of the study was irrefutable.

Example 2: Vocational Rehabilitation

A second example of logical auditors being very effective in nontraditional audit efforts centered on this social program that went back to the 1930s—a real "sacred cow," with huge expenditures.

All those we interviewed assured us this was a very beneficial program, with demonstrable results and statistics on rehabilitated clients. But what we really found was a Norumbega (see Rule of Thumb #6), a need to reexamine the base.

In truth, program counselors were "skating," that is they mainly selected the very easy cases to treat—alcoholics and clients with minor behavior problems. They considered the clients successfully rehabilitated if they went into new school programs or new jobs. What the counselors didn't reveal was the clients' recidivism rate. It was very high. Further, the new jobs, on closer inspection, proved to be at no higher pay than the jobs they held previous to entering the program.

And the people who needed help the most—the severely handicapped—were sloughed off into controlled-environment shelters and considered "helped."

Example 3: Military Reserve Training

I took a staff of about 15 auditors to a major reserve training site. We found over 18 percent of the trainees were being trained in specialties other than those officially assigned to them (their "MOSs"). Here, too, it was clear the operations had swerved from their intended path. And for years the written evaluations never reflected this. Auditors with "horse sense" and disciplined examination skills did the job.

Financial Statements—Through a Sort of "Shorthand—Describe What Was Spent, What Is Owed, and What the Organization's Worth Is, in Terms of Dollars, the Only Concrete Unit of Measure.

However, determining what was actually accomplished by an organization compared to what was intended is a more pressing need. Once that is determined, the next step is to ascertain that what was done, was done as economically as possible. But the most difficult step of all is to offer an opinion as to whether something ever should have been done in the first place, that maybe there were better things on which to spend the company's money.

That leads to some very heady considerations. At this point, the need for well-educated, renaissance auditors and analysts becomes more evident—auditors who can match wits with the CEOs they must convince.

Unhappily, accountants have a reputation for being stodgy thinkers—and even worse communicators—which is only partly justified.

But this is the place where we answer the question: "What effect did the audits have?" It's a tough one to answer, but it has to be done.

RULE OF THUMB #12
NO SURPRISES

Good Executives Neither Expect Surprises, Nor Spring Them on Their Staffs

Full and timely (that word again) disclosures are essential. Managers know not every situation turns out favorably; they can deal with problems, if they know about them. But they cannot, and should not, tolerate being taken off guard by new information, especially if it is unfavorable! The possible alternatives, presented in a timely manner, can be sensibly considered; the solution chosen and applied.

It Is Deceptively Easy to Make Decisions When Only One Choice Is Thought to Be Available

Often, there would be more choices, if CEOs took the time to communicate to the data gatherers what kind of information would be helpful to *them*.

The Solution

Don't allow the accountants to deliver information in their customary manner. As a general rule, most accountants are very "married" to their data accumulation techniques. They feel comfortable with the familiar. But, their data should be tailored and adapted to the CEO's needs in each situation.

RULE OF THUMB #13
THE GET-EVEN SYNDROME

Hidden Employee Hurts Can Damage or Destroy

Most CEOs would be astounded to discover how many on their immediate staff, or elsewhere in the organization, harbor resentment for some managerial or corporate misdeed allegedly done them. The all-too-human get-even syndrome can erupt in many ways, ranging from uncooperative behavior to outright sabotage.

Causal Situations

Causes for the get-even syndrome can range from the more common—raises, promotions, special assignments denied—to the less ordinary, such as the following:

Many organizations that have a telephone "hot line" available to employees and others wishing to report irregularities (particularly in government agencies) have been surprised by the number of complaints lodged. Many are frivolous—no more than telephonic graffiti venting contempt or irritation. But other messages revealed deep-seated grudges held against supervisors and/or the company in general.

How Do Such Potentially Treacherous Feelings Take Hold?

One source of resentment can be the seemingly harmless reassignment of office space. Perhaps larger quarters have become available; or, conversely, retrenchment requires employees to lower their on-the-job living standards. Festering grudges can follow such action, because the real pecking order in an organization has surfaced.

Unlike pay disparities, which are by and large a private matter and more easily hidden, office space broadcasts stature loud and clear. Reshuffling can cause a perceived loss of that stature. It often costs little more to maintain the status quo. Money saved by "cutting back" can be eaten up quickly through declining productivity.

Business Travel

Although travel for business quickly loses its appeal to those who must board one crowded airplane after another, the deskbound often harbor jealousy and resentment. And, business travelers often feel abused if they are away from home consistently but are still expected to put in all their office hours without letup.

Travel is a necessary and expensive business evil. Try to control it. Even out the assignments. Reimburse out-of-pocket expenses quickly. Give a little slack to the worker who came in on the red-eye and needs an extra hour's sleep the next morning.

Acting on the Problem

How do the network professionals help solve the get-even problem? Auditors should be on the alert to general organization morale. A little discreet listening can pinpoint most problems that have the potential for harm to the organization.

There are other indicators, too. Maybe quality is decreasing, or there are computer security breakdowns, or unexplained inventory shortages, or undue maintenance failures. These and many others can be warning signs of employees getting even with the company.

Contrary to Popular Opinion, People Don't Love to Hate Their Jobs

Most people, if given a choice, would choose a job they could look forward to every day. They would want to "whistle while they work," and idolize the company's leader as strong, capable and successful. They would rather point proudly to the company's product as the best that can be made.

Evidence Chrysler Corporation—the most beleaguered American automaker, beset with sabotage from within—when Lee Iacocca took the helm in the late 1970s. Even in the aftermath of sweeping pay and staff cuts, he created a loyal work force proud to have helped pull the company out of the clutches of defeat.

Public relations? Window dressing? Perceived reality *is* reality. You are what your employees believe you to be.

RULE OF THUMB #14
RIDING THE SHOULDER

Everyone Hopes the Authorities Will Catch the Culprits

Picture a line of autos on a busy weekend highway, waiting for an obstruction to be cleared that they may proceed to their Sunday destination. Everyone sits there patiently awhile.

Then, an almost palpable force descends. A few cars start riding the shoulder, trying to make some progress. And they do, but the rest of the motorists are agitatedly hoping a state patrolman is waiting farther up the road to give them a ticket and stop the flagrant flouting of the rules. Occasionally, a truck driver will assume the mantle of authority, positioning his rig so no one can pass. Other times, the shoulder riders move unobstructed, and more join them until the shoulder becomes a third lane, moving as slowly as the first two.

Apply the Analogy to Organizational Behavior

It is easy to draw parallels. If employees see others "riding the shoulder," perhaps taking unfair advantage by currying favor, or stealing ideas, or through shallow maneuvering, then resentment builds.

The organization becomes like the traffic jam. Perhaps someone at the same level, like the truck driver, assumes the authority to censure or stop the infractors. This never works. The atmosphere becomes charged with anger and resentment.

Perhaps workers perceive that management doesn't care; that, in fact, it seems the "shoulder riding" is working, paying off for those breaking the rules. Others become rule-breakers, too. Certain disgruntled workers become foot-draggers or out-and-out saboteurs—the final manifestation of the get-even syndrome. The system breaks down.

Those who choose none of the three options above—often the best and the brightest—will leave the company. Some will take corporate secrets with them, and feel justified in so doing.

Fair Review and Appraisal Policies, Not Just Written and Filed, But Dusted Off and Used, Along with Management's Unwavering Attention to Attitude and Morale, Will Help Avert the Get-Even Syndrome

Auditors can contribute by examining personnel records for possible wrongdoing, cover-ups, sloppy record keeping or data analysis, and missed reviews. Any or all of these can point to an organization "on the slide."

RULE OF THUMB #15
DON'T BELIEVE EVERYTHING YOU READ

Accountants' and Auditors' Reports May Not Be Saying What You Think They Are Saying. To Act Wisely, the CEO Needs Timely Information from Reliable Sources

This simple observation is not easily acted upon. CEOs often go without information on their company's operations they *should* have received from their professional support network. The information gatherers act as the judges of what will be gathered, and what to do with it once they have it.

Many Business Decisions Are Based in Part on Facts Garnered from Accounting and Audit Reports

Some of this "certified" data could lead an unsuspecting CEO into a wrong decision. Better communication with accountants and auditors can forestall calamity.

Certified Statements

One good example of where CEOs and accountants/auditors do not communicate sufficiently is when one company is considering the purchase of another. Often it is assumed they can rely heavily, if not exclusively, on certified audit statements (or those privately audited) for correct assessment of the value of the business under consideration. Not generally true.

For the Most Part, These Statements Portray a Business's Financial Condition as of a Particular Date. Missing, Though, Is Certain Critical Information, such as:

Sales. The market potential; a graph of previous sales; the selling picture and whether or not the company can produce what it needs for the right cost; salability of existing inventories; and on and on.

If it is a retail business, the obvious questions and answers are never in the account books. Considerations such as:

The community
The local employment scene
Housing developments
Population trends
Competition (in place or on the way)
Sales personnel (will they stay or go?)

Many of the above questions pertain to a manufacturing or service business as well.

The Bottom Line

Much of the missing information can be gathered, interpreted, and communicated by the CEO's professional support network. The process and logic involved is very similar to the recommendations in Part 2, "The Network and It's Swirling Currents," page 9. The CEO can organize and lead the attempt, while the network members conduct the information collection and evaluation. In addition to accountants and auditors, the team here might include lawyers, investigators, and the like.

Conclusion. Data and reports are only the materials of knowledge.

Thinking about them in a logical manner makes them useful. Accountants should spend more time asking CEOs what they want to know and less time preparing a lot of the trivia that bookkeepers amass. Analytical reporting of information cogent to the CEO—that is what is called for.

RULE OF THUMB #16
TRAINING IS NOT A REMOVABLE EXPENSE

Knowing Whom to Train and in What—The Difference Between Money Well Spent and Money Wasted

Most CEOs would agree that an "open secret" of good management is to hire top quality people, train them well, and give them an opportunity to do their jobs. Training should begin with top management, and sift throughout the staff.

Training in the Work Place:

Primarily, by example, augmented with management fiats: "You will do this; you shall not do that."

Second, by structured and semi-structured training courses for specific job classifications and professions.

As discussed earlier, training by example—management's showing the right attitudes and actions for workers to emulate—backed up with written policies spelling out the do's and don'ts, is of first importance.

What Other Training Is Important?

This question becomes more difficult to answer, as the need in business becomes greater for professionals and managers with a broad base of knowledge, not more narrowly trained technicians.

This is not to say that people should not become increasingly familiar with the specifics of their daily job assignments. But it is difficult to build a greater knowledge in a specific field in a person who lacks a strong foundation of general knowledge. And so it is that academic emphasis is moving back to the liberal arts.

In-House Training

As businesses recruit more and more liberal arts graduates, there will be a need for good, on-the-job training in specific skills. In the long run, this will probably be more efficient than the present scene. Today, business school grads come to the workplace with "ivory-tower" notions of business. They, too, need training and indoctrination in their employer's methods and applications.

The volume of training will not change measurably with the hiring of more liberal arts graduates. If you hire the brightest, most accomplished graduates, your company's training programs—if well-structured and taught to the graduates' level—can be relatively uncomplicated.

Trainers for junior executives can come from the ranks of middle- and upper-management. A well run program, with selected managers and professionals from inside spending so many hours a month teaching formal training classes and workshops, can be the least expensive and offer the best results. A good educational consultant and an in-house director of training should be able to establish and oversee the program nicely.

Formal Mentors

Even in smaller companies, whose management staffs number only in the single digits, in-house training is possible, through *formal mentor* programs. It has been shown that in the absence of formal mentors, new employees will latch on to informal mentors. Often their choice is not in the company's best interests.

It behooves the CEO to be sure there is a structure and a schedule for each new employee's crucial first months on the job, and a formal mentor to guide the new hire and offer instruction in the company's systems and style.

Outside Training

No CEO, or any other reasonably aware manager, needs to be told that outside training abounds. Seminars are big business nowadays, and let the buyer beware. Outside training courses should be selected with an eye to the company's *objectives* and *training budgets.* Set your training goals and budgets, to establish parameters for choosing among the many courses you will receive notification of during the year. A few hundred dollars here and there may not seem like a lot at the time, but it all adds up to zero if your managers attend a lot of "fluff" seminars thrown together in haste, or classes with subject matter not applicable to their work.

But do not be misled by these cautions. I have a definite bias *for* training, but the right training. Remember, too, that your existing managers may need more than classes advising them of the latest techniques in their specific craft or profession. Some need, literally, to "go back to school" and learn the basics: good writing, clear speaking, time management, personality skills. Every manager's training objectives should be established in writing each year, for that manager and for his or her entire department.

Training the CEO

Even the "top banana" can keep learning. One of this book's major themes is for managers to take charge of their professional support network, in particular the accountants and auditors who work for them.

One of the best ways to begin is by becoming more aware of the current thinking in these fields, through attending carefully selected seminars and workshops presented by accountants and auditors. (Check with your accountants for a recommendation.) This reciprocal training can help generalist CEOs better communicate with their specialists.

Middle Manager and General Work Force Training

Often, it is the most expendable employees who attend seminars and workshops, while the key people stay back at their desks, toiling away.

Many managers have never given training its due. When faced with training quotas to fill or budgets to spend, they often send the "low" people on their totem pole, the ones they can spare, to courses and workshops. Very little planning and consideration of how training could help meet department objectives ever goes into such decisions.

How Not to "How-To"

One glance at the hundreds of flyers and brochures that cross your desk for training will show they are heavily skewed toward "how-to" technical subjects: "How to Make Your Micros Work for You," "How to Handle Bankruptcies," "How to Advance Your Knowledge of Esoteric Sampling Methodology," "How to Better Deal with Construction Leases," and on and on.

Once you have decided what the company's managers need to learn "how to" do, don't stop there. Top management, not just its technicians, should also attend those courses with an emphasis on gaining an understanding of the basic powers that make or break an organization.

Learning to Think

The very notion that logic, and encouraging employees to think for themselves, needs a "hard sell" probably stems from a paucity of managerial analysis and practical problem solving courses—in college or out. Many managers feel less confident without specific direction and guidelines. In reality, however, they are on firm ground when what they do or suggest meets the high test of reason and plausibility. Unfortunately, most people would rather be told *what* to do than how to analyze a problem and decide for themselves.

Perhaps the problem stems from our educational system's emphasis on—and rewards for—the memorization and recitation of "facts." In business, too, we reward and promote those who can spew forth facts and details.

Consider the story told about Albert Einstein, who, when asked his telephone number, went to his city directory and looked it up. He is said to have explained that he preferred to use his mind for thinking, not as a storehouse of trivia for which there was ready reference.

Conclusion

Reward those who think, and whose actions are based on reason, and carried out within company policy and guidelines.

Emphasize training and improvement. Recognize those who do not simply "put in time" at a set number of training courses, but who put new ideas to work for the company. Hold them up as examples for others to follow.

Training does not have to take place on a campus, or in a hotel conference room. It can take place in the plant cafeteria, or company conference room. A training director, with the help of an educational consultant from a local college, can organize and lead a "militia" of company managers and professionals who serve as part-time teachers.

Training should be in the budget, and tied in to company objectives. When you stop learning and improving, you cease to exist.

RULE OF THUMB #17
STANDARDS ARE THE MARK OF A PROFESSION

The CEO Can Uncloak the Mystery of the Audit Process Through Knowing the Standards by Which It Is Governed

Congress, the courts, financial reporters, the general public, all are watching the auditors more closely than ever. Why?

Banks and savings and loans are in trouble. Why weren't the problems causing these troubles found by the auditors? The role of auditors in uncovering fraud is still unclear.

Tax accounting more and more becomes the domain of inventive and daring operators who search for new loopholes and techniques, "tax reform" notwithstanding.

According to the SEC, lawsuits against major public accounting firms have been settled to the tune of almost $200 million since 1980.

A close look at issues facing the accounting Standards Board, as of late 1986, shows that many remain unresolved. These include:

Pension plan accounting
Accounting for nonprofit organizations
Accounting for leases
Construction industry accounting
Repossession and reverse repossession
Accounting for business combinations
Utility accounting
Cash flow reporting
Accounting for computer software
Loan origination and acquisition fees
Accounting for futures
Collateralized mortgage obligations
Convertible debt and convertible securities

Standards: Eight main points

These secondary rules of thumb simplify and elucidate much of the detail contained in the standards:

1. Evidence, as it relates to audits of financial statements, should be persuasive. The GAO standards for audits involving compliance, economy, efficiency, and program results call for reasonable "assurance," translated, *evidence*.

2. Cost barrier: If unable to complete an audit properly, in full compliance with standards, because of fee restrictions, the auditor must disengage, or limit the opinion rendered.

3. Special concern is merited when dealing with cash and/or electronic data.

4. Auditors must exercise diligence to detect *gross error* or *misapplication*.

5. Auditors are admonished: *Do not deceive your readers!*

6. There is a critical difference between *accounting controls* (processes) and *administrative controls* (over major functions). Administrative controls are the more important.

7. All work must be *timely*. Nothing works well if the audit effort is not on-line.

8. The auditors' own judgment prevails above all else. They stand or fall on their own *independent opinions*.

Policy Handbook

An excellent example of an internal audit department's policy handbook can be found in Appendix A. It includes virtually all the important concepts in audit procedures, applicable standards, and many reporting techniques and requirements.

RULE OF THUMB #18
GOOD DATA ARE HARD TO FIND

The CEO Should Never Be Content with the Quantity and Quality of Information Received from the Network

The information that CEOs receive is normally filtered up through management layers. This is all well and good, but such filtering may take too much of the substance out of the information. Or, some of the substance may never get communicated at all, denying the CEO access to important facts.

Remember the Transom Theory of Accounting and Information Gathering

"Just drop the data through the window; our accountants will duly record it."

Some vital information will never come through the transom. Some that comes through will be discarded. Other information may be massaged and misrepresented. "Thinking auditors," who first ascertain what data the CEO needs before they begin checking it for relevance and accuracy, can help overcome this problem.

How Do I Know We're Doing a Good Job?

What constitutes a good or bad performance? In a profit-making organization, the bottom line is a good indicator, of course. But, should profits be higher? Is the profit figure inflated, due to some quirk? Are the profits increasing each year, and are they commensurate with the equity investment, or comparable with industry trends?

What is not easily determined, however, is whether or not the organization *maximized* its profits.

Conclusion

Examine closely the information you are now receiving and relying on. Look for gaps. Meet with your network and discuss how they can draw a complete, regular picture for you without the organization falling prey to a data overload and "spreadsheetitis."

RULE OF THUMB #19
GOOD WRITING IS THE SIGN OF AN ORGANIZED MIND

There Is No Trick to Good Business Prose—It Results from High Standards, Hard Practice, and One-on-One Capable Supervision

Many CEOs have learned how to get their messages across, in written and spoken form. In many cases, the ability to communicate set the achiever apart, and smoothed the climb to the top.

It never hurts to brush up. The rules of thumb that follow will help you refresh your style. Or, give them as guidelines to the staffers whose weighty prose you must suffer through daily.

Simple and Direct

Hold these two words as your guide. Written business communication—be it memo, letter or report—is at its best when it achieves an economy of style. Know what you want to say (organize your thoughts) and set your ideas forth in clear, uncluttered sentences.

Techniques Can Be Learned, But the Willingness to Improve Must Come First

Good writing requires concentration and—often, at the start— revision, revision, revision. With practice, clear prose can flow in the first draft. But even the world's most skilled writers put aside their work for later review.

Think *Before* You Write

Know your facts. Get a fix on your reader. Know what you want to say and why.

Decide on *main* and *secondary* themes; set them firmly in your mind. Write them at the top of your paper, or screen, and refer back to them. If you stray from the main purpose, get back on track.

Do some mental filing of your facts. How do they fit? If it helps, draw a diagram for your use before you begin.

Which facts are important? You can irritate a learned reader by writing the obvious, and annoy all others by not sufficiently explaining yourself.

Use White Space

Pity the executive faced with volumes to read, study, understand, act on.

Compose Your Writing

Consider Beethoven. First came the simple musical theme. Dom, da, dom, dom. Then the theme is enlarged, first with the woodwinds, next with the violins, then brass, then all together. Underlying themes are brought up. Then the composition is rounded out with the whole orchestra. Add some cymbals and drums from time to time to interest and arouse the reader.

Brief, but Brilliant

The shorter the message, the harder it is to put succinctly. There is more risk of conveying the wrong impression with a few words than with a dissertation. Politicians are forever trying to explain away a misunderstood "off the cuff" remark made in a speech or in response to a reporter's question.

Do not underestimate the effect, however, of short reports, letters or notes. I remember clearly, even after 20 years, because it was that good, a message I received from the Secretary of the Department of Health and Human Services (then HEW) in response to my written request. I asked what he thought about an audit approach to a study of the Medicaid programs in 17 states. The answer came back, in thick pencil scrawl, on my original query: "Add Mass!"

Direct and to the point. In two words he accepted the suggested approach and added a directive to review the operations of the State of Massachusetts to the other states in the study. Sometimes that is all that is needed.

What You Cannot Explain, You've Done in Vain

Narrative reports portray the essence of the work of auditors, accountants, and others. If the work cannot be reported in plain, understandable English, then that work is mostly wasted. At the very least, poor communication wastes *time,*

time spent explaining in person what a well-written report should have accomplished.

Legal documents, insurance policies, computer manuals, and, unhappily, most audit reports, are not generally easy-to-read. The auditor's investigative reports, often are no more than observations dictated onto a tape and transcribed verbatim, without organization or a format the reader can follow.

Back to Basics

It bears repeating that, if CEOs desire clear, useful reports and manuals, either for in-house purposes or directed to the customer, they must make sure they have a literate network.

Referring back to training needs, don't overlook good courses to help your executives dispense with cluttered writing styles. Often, the very educated must be sent back to basics to learn clear communication.

The Academic Connection

Explore the possibility of bringing in a "writing consultant" from a local college or university, to conduct business writing workshops for your management team. The money spent will be made up in time, efficiency, and fewer incidences of "crossed wires."

RULE OF THUMB #20
FOLLOW THE ORDERLY LINE

A Sense of Order and Fair Play Promotes Harmony in the Workplace. Destroy It at Your Peril

Most people are remarkably patient and decent, considering the stresses to which they are subjected in their daily personal and work lives. They will wait in lines at the supermarket, at the theater, or on the highway. And at the office, for the most part, they are willing to wait "their turn" for raises and promotions.

But let those patient people notice others "bucking" the line, and getting away with it, and they become an unruly mob. It has been said the Japanese are so genteel because of the country's population density. Imagine the pressures that would explode in such highly populated areas as downtown Tokyo, if they were not relieved by consideration and patience.

In the Workplace

How then, does this rule of thumb affect organizational management?

If managers (or others) perceive they can advance by adroit socializing or "buttering up" the right superiors, then organizational order can be upset. The workings of the internal control mechanism and the basic organizational integrity are at risk. Some may adopt a get-even attitude; others might become disenchanted with the atmosphere and seek employment elsewhere.

The Control Connection

There is an important connection here to the reliability of internal controls. Auditors must be alert to the organizational order (or breakdown thereof) when they discover inaccuracies, fudging, or abuse. An organization that appears to shun the "straight and narrow" in both action and attitude is a vulnerable one. If nothing else, managers may feel justified in taking improper actions to equalize their chances for upward movement. Tit for tat. Human resources management becomes a firefighting brigade, rather than a vehicle to enhance the contributions of employees.

RULE OF THUMB #21
GUARD AGAINST WHITE-COLLAR CRIME

White-Collar Crime Is a $200 Billion Problem That Affects Everyone

Wrongful activities committed by the use of misrepresentation, guile, or deception to obtain something of value, prevent loss, or obtain personal or business advantage, often in violation of a fiduciary relationship.

Who Are Its Perpetrators?

Almost anyone, from every social and economic stratum in society.

The Criminal Equation

If all the components necessary for a criminal act are present, there is a high likelihood there will be a crime.
   There must be:

   An object at which wrongdoing is directed: Target
   An individual with a reason to attack: Motive
   An ability to get in proximity to attack: Access
   Circumstances favorable to a purpose: Opportunity

Target + Motive + Access + Opportunity = The Criminal Equation

When we talk about fraud, abuse, and other white-collar crime, we are not just dealing with the breakdown of systems of accounting and their related internal controls in a technical sense. We are looking at a breakdown of basic human behaviors and of the individual's interactions with business and society as a whole. And, as much of this book highlights in various ways, one cannot always separate the intrinsic technical elements from the more subjective, human elements.

Similarly, one cannot deal with fraud and abuse as a separate problem. This whole area is one of vast disagreement as to causes and remedies.

When you encounter a criminal act, you are forced to face the feelings and personalities of people, as well as the forces (economic and otherwise) that move them. Employees, entrepreneurs, managers, CEOs, their families, and more make up the cast of characters. In this cast are the "villains," always scheming and planning to commit a wrong. Then there are the "heroes," who may have motive, access and opportunity, but would never commit an unlawful or immoral act.

But the rest of the cast falls somewhere in between; and given one or more of the factors of the equation, might be capable of committing a wrong. The criminal equation governs.

True internal controls can remove the opportunities and access for white collar crime. And, as this book has stressed throughout, organizational *attitude* is a key factor in eliminating the motives.

Wherever possible, companies must reward and encourage positive contributions, and swiftly handle negative behavior. This is not just a moralistic truism, but a practical recommendation that leads to greater economies and profits.

Out of Touch

Our present society is a much less "personal" one than what it was 100, even 50 years ago. People are on the move. They hide in big houses behind trees, often never knowing their neighbors except to nod "hello." Mothers work, children go to day-care centers and after-school programs, and the neighborhood as the setting of daily social interaction is all but gone.

Hence, the deterrent of the "community watchdog" no longer exists. Heavy social pressures that once might have prevented criminal activity are not present. False advertising, cheating, and deceptive merchandising are accepted facts of life.

Computers Lend Anonymity

Add to this picture an important new element: computers. The result: a business world more vulnerable than ever before. Computers add, exponentially, to the concerns about white-collar crime.

It is often impossible to determine *who* made the entries—right or wrong, honest or fraudulent, or just mischievous—lending anonymity to the perpetrator.

As first the industrial age, then the space age, changed the way we do business, the information age requires of management new awareness and constant vigilance. Never before has a trusted network of professionals been so important.

RULE OF THUMB #22
THE HIGH ROAD/THE LOW ROAD

Be a Firm, Even-Tempered Manager. Show Some Humor

Only the most agile can walk both roads at the same time, and those who can are also the most effective. This concept is rarely reviewed in a hard-nosed, administrative sense.

Chief Executive Officers Set the Tone

They should insist, on one hand, that everyone on their staff pursue excellence in their work, that the goals of the organization be honestly and unfailingly sought.

The CEOs capable of directing in such a manner, with an earnest attitude and even disposition, and who can still sea-son the organizational soup with humor and fun, are the real superstars.

The Right Attitude at the Top Is Contagious

Convey the message that everything you—and the organization—are doing is a "big deal." Do your best to stay in control of this important effort. But keep in mind that what one does rarely is a big deal, over time. The Greeks based their "Serio/Comic" philosophies on this simple, but powerful, point.

In Organizational Terms

The people in an organization will benefit from a steady, even-handed CEO who can sort out what is important and relevant, and what is not; who doesn't take himself too seriously, and who is approachable with new ideas and creative criticism.

Specific Benefits

This approach helps create integrity and the pursuit of excellence that is vital for top performance. But nothing says that *great management cannot be enjoyable.* Staff members like to do a good honest day's work and feel productive. If there is a little humor thrown in, what harm?

Staff members will in one form or another get even with harsh executives. Yet, over and over again it has been demonstrated that the solid, innovative, and winning organizations—from sports dynasties, to long-running entertainment shows, to solid corporations—are those whose members respect and even like their top leaders, leaders who can walk the two roads at the same time.

Look for the leader who never has to ask for overtime from the staff; they automatically know when extra effort is needed, and give it gladly. These are the organizations that experience the least fraud and abuse.

Accepting Organizational Misfits

In these days of fast-moving style, changing mores, and amazing new technology, there should be room in every organization for extraordinary people: those who may not quite fit in the regular office career or management hierarchy.

These are the individuals who, when encouraged or just left alone, will present you with the new products and ideas, or contest the Norumbegas in the company's systems and style. This certainly applies to audit and accounting methods as well as new product development.

For example, one might well take the position, as does the newly emerging Chinese accounting society, that in most cases there is nothing particularly solid or sacred about accrued expenses or deferred income. Why not, ask, "just write them off as they occur?"

Chances are the beginning and closing totals in an ongoing business have the same relationship to the rest of the accounting balances. So, from a practical "materiality" viewpoint, nothing is served by manipulating them in a "bookish" endeavor. In truth, most auditing practitioners who serve small businesses just enter these items as expenses or income as they occur.

General Observations

The more one reads about the emerging superstar companies or the older, solid performers who keep getting better, the more apparent are the common denominators in their success. And I refer to well-known firms that have received much play in the media—firms like Remington Shaver Company, Hughes Aircraft, The Limited, Inc., Dayton Power and Light, and so on.

Their success seems to stem from flexible timeliness in business decisions and product introductions, and hands-on CEOs who are not afraid to set a tone of enjoyable management, or to give their managers free rein (once the company's ethics and objectives have been set forth). This does not in any way detract from solid administrative control and methods. Rather, this attitude fortifies the company's defenses against the get-even syndrome. It also makes it responsive to changing market trends and new technologies.

Responsible, Productive Employees Thrive in an Atmosphere of Enjoyable Management

There is nothing weak or frivolous about this managerial precept. Rather, it is a strength and a resource upon which to draw in good times and bad.

This, plus the CEO's commitment to ongoing training, and receptiveness to new ideas and methods, should be transmitted to the network of accountants and auditors.

4

Orchestrating the Network

HOW THE NETWORK WORKS

Just how does the network come together? How do all the players learn, and execute, their parts?

The CEO occupies the center of the vortex. Through participating with and directing the various forces, the CEO can harness the power of the swirling currents for the good of the organization.

Organizations function best when their staff and operational divisions work as a whole body, not a loose collection of disparate parts.

Be generous with rewards for cooperative, executive attitudes and behavior. Do not avoid the less pleasant task of reprimanding those who pursue their own interests. Respond to both behaviors in a visible and timely fashion.

Conceptual Model—Audit Elements of the Network

Following is a description of the effective combination of the audit elements of the network. For the purpose of illustration, the organization discussed is an "ordinary" business, if any business can be said to be ordinary, or predictable.

External Controls

The CPA's main objectives are to certify to the world at large that (1) the statements as reported by management fairly represent the assets, liabilities, expenses, and income for the period in question; and (2) the accounting methods used were consistent with that of the previous period. They would also like to be able to state that their tests were timely and dependable, and that internal controls were solid enough to support their confidence in these examinations.

Internal Controls

The internal auditor's principle activities are (1) testing of the internal control mechanisms; (2) timely examinations of system adequacy so that periodic accounting analyses are useful and reliable; and (3) testing to assure that operations are efficient and that the company's assets are secure. Here their responsibilities go beyond certifying that ending balances are correct, to analyzing whether the right amount was spent in the right areas.

What becomes evident is that these two network parts must really join forces in common endeavor, both in the data they check and how they check it. To illustrate:

1. *Inventories.* The ending total is only one area of focus. There are a number of related operations that occur all during the year.

Warehousing methods could be inefficient. Theoretically, a heroic effort at year end could produce a correct closing balance verified by scientific and reliable counting methods; and the ledgers could be adjusted to compensate for errors made in the prior 12 months. But internal auditors, with timely testing and observations, can catch and stop poor warehouse methods, such as damage due to sloppy handling, spoilage due to poor storage techniques, or exorbitant shipping cost due to inefficient carrier tie-ins.

By coordinating their testing and surveying techniques, the two audit forces can complement and strengthen each other's work with a minimum of duplication.

2. *Accounts Payable.* The CPAs want to know if the ending balance as shown in the ledgers is correct. So do the internal auditors, but they also want to know if the procurement techniques were efficient. Were purchases made only for the amounts needed and as close as possible to the time they were needed, or was there a combination of stockpiles and shortages? Were all possible discounts taken and were company procurement policies followed? Were decisions whether to buy from outside or produce internally made correctly?

Here again, the logical meshing and cooperation of audit forces benefits both audit functions and the company as well. But unless management steps in early, before the process is established, and insists on close audit interactions, then it only happens to the extent that the chief auditors, of both camps, take it upon themselves to make it happen.

Working Together

If we accept the premise that management attitudes and organizational style are crucial to the reliability of the internal control system, then it would follow that it is pivotal for the internal auditors to tell the external auditors what they need to know—and what the internal auditors are best able to determine through their on-site and on-line presence.

The CEO must insist that the internal and external staffs have a vehicle for the *timely* exchange of questions or uncertainties of a material nature.

The principles are the same no matter what the business. Timely auditing means having your staff doing the testing when and where it is needed. Determining when and where is a management function governed by how constant, or mercurial, the business is.

Again, the emphasis should be on checking only what is current, dispensing with old material. Sampling should be done on a "moving target" basis so that the picture that results is a sharp, well-focused image of current operations.

Find someone with an honest sense of humor, the ability to distinguish the trivial from the important, native intelligence, and the drive and stamina to keep it all going, and you have the makings of a great executive.

APPENDIX A

Group Health Cooperative of Puget Sound

Internal Audit Department

Policy Handbook

Foreword

This Handbook reflects the policies and procedures which have been developed internally through extensive review and analysis of the particular needs of Internal Audit. Appropriate recognition is given to fundamental Auditing Standards coming from professional sources.

This Policy Handbook is distributed to members of GHC - Management and Internal Audit - for their guidance and use. It sets forth major policies on the broad technical aspects of auditing.

VIRGINIA MOODY
Director, Internal Audit

September 16, 1985

TABLE OF CONTENTS

INTERNAL AUDIT CHARTER

PURPOSE:

To establish the scope and activities of the Internal Audit function within Group Health Cooperative (GHC) in accordance with prescribed Audit Standards.

NATURE:

GHC Internal Audit is an independent appraisal activity within the Cooperative. It functions as a service to management by continually measuring and evaluating the effectiveness of the organization's internal operational controls and the accuracy of the accounting/financial records.

OBJECTIVE:

The objective of Internal Audit is to help management discharge its responsibilities effectively. In this regard, Internal Audit searches for causes of inefficiencies or uneconomical practices so that management may correct these practices. Internal Audit furnishes management with analyses, appraisals, recommendations and pertinent comments concerning activities reviewed.

The attainment of this overall objective involves reviewing accounting, financial, other operations and systems, both manual and electronic, to determine for top management that...

- assets are properly accounted for and safeguarded from losses.
- management plans, policies and procedures are followed and carried out effectively and efficiently.
- adequate accounting and managerial controls exist... and function properly in relation to the organization's objectives.
- recommendations are implemented for appropriate improvements in control.
- timely, useful and reliable data exist for decision making.

RESPONSIBILITY AND AUTHORITY:

The responsibilities of Internal Audit within GHC are established by this Charter in accordance with prescribed Auditing Standards.

Internal Audit has the authority to inspect records and property at any location relevant to the subject under review. It is expected that departments or activities under review will provide every possible assistance to facilitate the progress of the audit.

The Director of Internal Audit has direct liaison with the Chief Executive Officer (CEO) and independent access to all other levels of management. The Director will submit to the CEO an annual audit of work plan for approval. The CEO will receive all final Audit Reports. Each year a report of Internal Audit activities will be presented to the Management Issues Committee and the Board of Trustees for their information.

In order to avoid duplication of effort, all audit effort will be coordinated. To this end, the Director of Internal Audit will coordinate its audit work with that of the external auditors.

In accordance with Auditing Standards, Internal Audit has no direct responsibility for or authority over any of the activities reviewed. An Internal Audit review and appraisal, therefore, does not in any way relieve managers in the organization from their regular responsibilities assigned to them.

INDEPENDENCE:

Independence is essential to the effectiveness of Internal Audit function. This independence is established and maintained by organizational status and objectivity.

Organizational Status:
- Internal Audit reports to and is supported by the Vice-President, Management Resources. This reporting and administrative relationship assures a broad range of audit coverage and adequate consideration of effective corrective action on audit findings and recommendations.

Objectivity:
- Objectivity is critical to the independence of the audit function. Auditors therefore, should not develop and install procedures, prepare records or engage in other activities which could compromise their independence.

- Auditor's objectivity does not preclude determining and recommending standards of control to be applied in the development of system - manual and/or electronic - or the reviewing of procedures before they are implemented.

_____
Chief Executive Officer

_____
Date

POLICY HANDBOOK

AUDITING STANDARDS INTRODUCTION

CHAPTER 1

1.00   **INTRODUCTION**
1.10   **OBJECTIVES**
1.20   **SUMMARY OF STANDARDS**

1.00   INTRODUCTION

Professional Auditing Standards are formalized criteria used in the practice of auditing. This handbook sets forth the particular Audit Standards that will be followed by the Internal Audit Department in the auditing of accounting, financial and other systems/operations, both manual and electronic, within Group Health Cooperative (GHC). These Standards are based on the formal auditing Standards promulgated by the Institute of Internal Auditors, the American Institute of CPAs and the General Accounting Office.

1.10   OBJECTIVES

The primary objectives of these Standards are to ensure that:

    ...   audit work accomplishes the purpose of the function,

    ...   audit resources are used effectively and efficiently,

    ...   audit work conforms to generally accepted auditing standards for the professional practice of Internal Auditing, and

    ...   all audit effort is coordinated - internal and external.

1.20   SUMMARY OF STANDARDS

The following Audit Standards are the basis for audit coverage and operations within GHC. They are divided into four parts:

    ...   General,

    ...   Examination and Evaluation,

    ...   Reporting, and

    ...   Supplemental Standards on Auditing Computer-based Systems,

The above Standards will be discussed in subsequent chapters, two - five.

POLICY HANDBOOK

GENERAL AUDITING STANDARDS

CHAPTER 2

2.00	**INTRODUCTION**
2.10	**SUMMARY OF GENERAL STANDARDS**
2.20	**SCOPE OF AUDIT WORK**
2.20.1	Financial/Compliance
2.20.2	Economy/Efficiency
2.20.3	Program Results
2.20.4	The Computer Environment
2.30	**COORDINATION WITH EXTERNAL AUDITORS**
2.40	**QUALIFICATIONS OF AUDITORS**
2.50	**INDEPENDENCE**
2.60	**DUE PROFESSIONAL CARE**

2.00   INTRODUCTION

Within the codification of Auditing Standards certain ones are referred to as 'General Standards'. These particular Standards are concerned with the quality of performance and the judgements that auditors exercise in their professional work.

In recognizing that individual judgement is exercised and required in the performance of audit work, members of the Internal Audit staff have the responsibility to conduct themselves in such a manner that their integrity is not open to question. It is expected that all auditors shall promote the highest possible Internal Audit Standards within GHC.

This chapter discusses these General Standards.

2.10   SUMMARY OF GENERAL STANDARDS

2.10.1   Scope of Audit Work

The scope of audit work encompasses independent appraisals of diverse functions, activities or programs within GHC to determine whether:

...   accepted policies and procedures are followed,

...   established standards are met,

...   assets are safeguarded,

...   resources are used efficiently and economically,

POLICY HANDBOOK

GENERAL AUDITING STANDARDS
CHAPTER 2

2.10   **SUMMARY OF GENERAL STANDARDS** (Cont...)

     2.10.1   Scope of Audit Work (Cont...)

     ...   planned programs are accomplished effectively, and

     ...   the organization's objectives are being achieved.

     In determining the scope of a particular audit, Internal Audit should consider management's need regarding the results of the audit.

     2.10.2   Coordination with External Auditors

     Internal and external audit work should be coordinated to ensure adequate audit coverage and to minimize the duplication of effort.

     2.10.3   Qualifications of Auditors

     The Auditor(s) assigned to perform the audit must either possess, or collectively possess, adequate professional proficiency for the tasks required.

     2.10.4   Independence

     In matters relating to audit work, an independent attitude should be maintained by Internal Audit.

     2.10.5   Due Professional Care

     Due professional care is to be used in conducting the audit and in preparing related reports.

2.20   **SCOPE OF AUDIT WORK**

The scope of internal auditing work, as discussed in this Standard encompasses the various types of audit work to be performed. Audit coverage consists of examinations into:

     ...   financial/compliance,

     ...   economy/efficiency,

     ...   program results, and

POLICY HANDBOOK

GENERAL AUDITING STANDARDS
CHAPTER 2

2.20   SCOPE OF AUDIT WORK (Cont...)

...   the computer environment.

In developing and maintaining a comprehensive audit program, it is essential to determine the scope of the audit. This involves planning specific audit objectives for each assignment. Audit scope should be tailored to each function, activity or program according to individual circumstances, management needs, overall audit capacity and work priorities. In many cases, this 'tailoring' approach will result in audits that are mixtures of various thrusts of coverage.

2.20.1   Financial/Compliance

A major aspect of Internal Audit's mission is to provide a reasonable degree of assurance that dollars are expended properly and for purposes for which they are designated. This work, largely performed through a financial/compliance audit, is aimed at determining whether:

...   effective control over revenues, expenditures, assets, and/or liabilities is maintained;

...   resources are accounted for properly;

...   financial reports contain accurate, reliable, and useful financial data and are fairly presented;

...   applicable policies, procedures and/or regulations are followed; and

...   management directives are still valid to meet current organizational objectives.

Though the concept of 'compliance' is normally linked with financial coverage, areas can involve legal and program requirements that are removed from strictly fiscal concerns.

2.20.2   Economy/Efficiency

Internal Audit's mission also includes determining whether GHC's diverse operating systems are conducted economically and efficiently.

POLICY HANDBOOK

GENERAL AUDITING STANDARDS

CHAPTER 2

2.20.2   Economy/Efficiency (Cont...)

This type of audit work focuses on the adequacy of management controls over the use of resources... management of employees, money and materials... and emphasizes the search for causes of any inefficiencies or uneconomical practices so that management may correct them.

2.50.3   Program Results

Audit work can also involve determining whether 'planned programs' are effectively achieving desired results.

These types of review, aimed at the evaluation of program or activity results, determine whether desired benefits are being obtained. Considerations are:

> ...   relevance and validity of criteria used;

> ...   appropriateness of methods followed by the entity to evaluate the effectiveness in achieving program results;

> ...   accuracy of data accumulated; and

> ...   reliability of results obtained.

2.20.4   The Computer Environment

With the advent of computerized information another thrust has been added to the role expected of the auditor. In this regard, the AICPA in December, 1974 and GAO in March, 1979 issued additional audit standards for auditing computer-based systems. A full discussion of this area is covered in Chapter five of this handbook, entitled "Supplemental Computer Related Standards".

2.30   COORDINATION WITH EXTERNAL AUDITORS

In carrying out the responsibilities of the audit function, it is essential that all audit effort is coordinated to ensure proper audit coverage with minimum duplication of effort.

POLICY HANDBOOK

GENERAL AUDITING STANDARDS

CHAPTER 2

2.30   **COORDINATION WITH EXTERNAL AUDITORS** (Cont...)

To this end, Internal Audit will coordinate its audit efforts with the external auditors. This coordination will involve:

      ...   periodic meetings to discuss matters of mutual interest,

      ...   access to each other's audit programs and workpapers,

      ...   exchange of audit reports and management letters, and

      ...   in some instances, assisting in the financial verification program.

2.40   QUALIFICATIONS OF AUDITORS

The third General Standard places upon the Internal Auditing Department and each Internal Auditor the responsibility for professional and technical proficiency.   The Internal Auditing staff should have collectively the necessary knowledge and skills essential to auditing within GHC.

In addition to basic auditing proficiency - auditing standards, procedures and techniques - emphasis is placed on obtaining such specialized skills as accounting, electronic data processing, statistics, economics, finance, etc. to meet audit responsibilities. These and other skills may be possessed by staff members or by consultants to the staff.

Further, it is the Internal Audit Department's policy to draw on the diverse skills and expertise of health care specialists employed in other units of GHC, when necessary, to achieve the objectives of a particular audit, and when, the assistance required can be furnished by a reliable, unbiased source.   If necessary skills cannot be obtained, audit objectives will be modified accordingly.

This standard also recognizes that current developments and improvements are continually taking place in accounting and EDP areas. In this regard, auditors have a responsibility to maintain their proficiency through education, understanding and the application of new pronouncements on accounting principles and auditing procedures developed by authoritative bodies.

POLICY HANDBOOK

GENERAL AUDITING STANDARDS

CHAPTER 2

2.50   INDEPENDENCE

The fourth General Standard provides that in all matters relating to audit work, an independent mental attitude is critical. Internal Auditors are to perform audits in such a manner that they are able to make honest and objective judgements... not subordinating their judgement to that of others.

Staff assignments should be made so that potential and actual conflicts of interest and bias are avoided as well as assignments should be rotated periodically; persons transferred to or temporarily engaged by the Internal Auditing Department should not be assigned to audit those activities they had previously performed until a reasonable period of time has elapsed; and, the results of internal auditing work - the related audit report - should be reviewed before it is released to provide reasonable assurance that the work was performed objectively.

The organization also has a responsibility to ensure that auditors have the ability to form independent and objective conclusions. Therefore, it is essential in accomplishing audit objectives that there be no:

> ...   improper interference or influence over audit procedures, selection of activities to be examined, or audit results; and

> ..   denied access to records or other sources of information.

2.60   DUE PROFESSIONAL CARE

The fifth General Standard calls for Internal Auditors to exercise good judgement and skill appropriate to the complexities of audit being performed. This implies that Internal Auditors should be alert to the possibility of intentional wrongdoing, errors and omissions, inefficiency, waste, ineffectiveness and conflicts of interest. The auditor must observe due care both in field work and in reporting findings. To this end, the internal auditor should consider:

> ...   the extent of audit work needed to achieve audit objectives;

> ...   the relative materiality or significance of matters to which procedures are applied;

POLICY HANDBOOK

GENERAL AUDITING STANDARDS

CHAPTER 2

2.60   **DUE PROFESSIONAL CARE** (Cont...)

...   the adequacy and effectiveness of internal controls; and

...   the cost of auditing in relation to potential benefits.

While due care implies reasonable care and competence, it does not mean infallibility or extraordinary performance. The auditor is required to conduct examinations and verifications to a reasonable extent.

POLICY HANDBOOK

EXAMINATION AND EVALUATION STANDARDS

CHAPTER 3

3.00   **INTRODUCTION**
3.10   **SUMMARY OF GENERAL STANDARDS**
3.20   **PLANNING**
3.20.1   The Audit Work Plan
3.20.2   The Audit Assignment
3.30   **SUPERVISION**
3.40   **LEGAL AND REGULATORY REQUIREMENTS**
3.50   **INTERNAL CONTROL**
3.60   **EVIDENCE**

3.00   INTRODUCTION

An audit framework pertaining to the planning and performance of audit work will be developed which is consistent with the Standards for the Professional Practice of Internal Auditing adopted by the Institute of Internal Auditors.

3.10   SUMMARY OF EXAMINATION AND EVALUATION STANDARDS

...   Work is adequately planned.

...   Auditors are properly supervised.

...   Reviews are made of compliance with legal and regulatory requirements.

...   Evaluations are made of internal controls to assess the extent they can be relied upon to ensure accurate information; to ensure compliance with laws and regulations; to provide for efficient and effective operations; and to safeguard assets.

...   Sufficient, competent, relevant and useful information is obtained to afford a reasonable basis for the auditor's findings and recommendations.

3.20   PLANNING

Proper planning ensures that audit effort is directed at significant activities within GHC. Key planning concerns include:

...   identifying areas of risk/exposure;

POLICY HANDBOOK

EXAMINATION AND EVALUATION STANDARDS
CHAPTER 3

3.20   PLANNING (Cont...)

...   ranking auditable areas according to criteria;

...   allocating appropriate resources based on audit scope; and

...   matching professional skills to the planned audit activity.

3.20.1   The Audit Work Plan

A yearly audit plan will be developed from management input, findings by the external auditor and concerns noted by the internal auditors. The following factors are criteria used to determine the frequency and priority of scheduled audits.

...   Newness, changed conditions or sensitivity of the function or activity,

...   Dollar magnitude and duration...relative vulnerability,

...   Governmental regulations,

...   Prior audit experience - coverage and results,

...   Results of other evaluations, e.g., external auditors, accreditation reviews, etc., and

...   Availability of audit resources.

3.20.2   The Audit Assignment

Special investigative assignments dealing with targets of opportunity may come up in addition to the above reviews. Determination to perform a special review will be made by the Director of Internal Audit.

The individual audit assignment also involves planning and includes assembling basic preliminary information (the survey) necessary to develop specific audit objectives and audit programs. At GHC where prior internal audit experience is lacking survey work is extensive. It will involve significant time and effort identifying and documenting an activity or function.

POLICY HANDBOOK

EXAMINATION AND EVALUATION STANDARDS

CHAPTER 3

3.20.2   The Audit Assingment (Cont...)

The audit program which is an audit guideline contains specific audit steps to be followed by the auditor such as computer assisted techniques or statistical sampling. In this manner the audit program is used to:

> ...   communicate audit objectives and steps to all assigned auditors;
>
> ...   help control work; and
>
> ...   provide a permanent record of the audit plan.

3.30   <u>SUPERVISION</u>

The second Examination and Evaluation Standard places the responsibility for appropriate audit supervision on the Director of Internal Auditing. Supervision is a continuing process, beginning with planning the audit assignment and endidng with its conclusion. In this manner, questions and/or errors in audit work are identified on a timely basis.

Supervisory review of audit work should be documented.   Major review concerns are:

> ...   conformance with audit standards;
>
> ...   following the audit programs (with deviations where justified and authorized) and resolution of any open questions;
>
> ...   adequate working papers to support findings;
>
> ...   adequately developed findings for reporting purposes; and
>
> ...   the overall accomplishment of audit objectives.

The supervisory auditor has an overriding professional responsibility to ensure that the total product of each audit assignment meets the full measure of professional adequacy.

POLICY HANDBOOK
EXAMINATION AND EVALUATION STANDARDS
CHAPTER 3

3.40   LEGAL AND REGULATORY REQUIREMENTS

The third Examination and Evaluation Standard provides that any appropriate legal and regulatory requirements that have direct bearing or significant impact on the specific objectives of an audit assignment should be reviewed for compliance. Laws, regulations, or related material should be identified in the audit program.

3.50   INTERNAL CONTROL

The fourth Examination and Evaluation Standard, deals with the auditor's responsibility for determining how much reliance can be placed on the organization's internal control system to ensure accurate information, compliance with applicable laws and regulations, promote economy and efficiency, and produce effective results. Findings from this evaluation help the auditor determine how much detailed examination work must be performed to achieve audit objectives.

Internal control includes management's plan of organization and all the coordinate methods and measures adopted to safeguard assets, check the accuracy and reliability of accounting data, promote operational efficiency, and encourage adherence to prescribed managerial policies. The characteristics of internal control include:

> ...   a plan of organization that provides segregation of duties appropriate for safeguarding resources;

> ...   a system of authorization and recording procedures adequate to provide effective accounting control over assets, liabilities, revenues and expenses;

> ...   an organizational system of practices to be followed in performance of duties of each separate yet connecting functions;

> ...   personnel of a quality commensurate with their responsibilities; and

> ...   an effective system of internal review.

Internal review is an important part of internal control, and it is the policy of Internal Audit to take full advantage of the results of all internal review. In performing audits the auditor will:

POLICY HANDBOOK

EXAMINATION AND EVALUATION STANDARDS

CHAPTER 3

3.50   **INTERNAL CONTROL** (Cont...)

...   look into the work performed by other reviewers;

...   consider the nature and extent of such work, and

...   decide to what extent it can be relied upon to ensure that other aspects of internal control are functioning properly.

3.60   **EVIDENCE**

The fifth and last Examination and Evaluation Standard provides that sufficient, competent, relevant and useful evidence (information) should be obtained to afford a rational and logical basis for the auditor's findings and recommendations.   Considerable amount of the audit effort consists in obtaining, examining, and evaluating evidential matter.

Evidence needed to support audit findings may be:

...   physical evidence obtained by observation, photograph, or similar means;

...   testimonial evidence obtained by interviewing or taking statements from involved persons;

...   documentary evidence extracted from accounting records, etc.; and

...   analytical evidence secured by analysis of information obtained.

POLICY HANDBOOK

AUDIT STANDARDS - REPORTING

CHAPTER 4

4.00	**PREAMBLE**
4.10	**PURPOSE**
4.20	**SUMMARY OF REPORTING STANDARDS**
4.30	**ADVANCE DISCUSSIONS**
4.40	**THE FORMAL REPORT**
4.50	**PRIORITY ACTION MEMORANDUM**
4.60	**THE LETTER REPORT**
4.70	**THE ANNUAL REPORT**

4.00   PREAMBLE

The audit process in an evolving, developing process within Group Health. As such, Internal Audit will modify, as needed, its reporting standards in order to respond more effectively to the environment.   Internal Audit will try, whenever practical, to ensure that senior management is aware of any modification affecting their involvement. All revisions will be in writing and distributed to appropriate personnel.

4.10   PURPOSE

The following audit guidelines set forth the reporting of information to management regarding audit findings. This communication will be handled in a manner that meets Reporting Standards as prescribed in the Auditing Standards of the Institute of Internal Auditors (IIA) and the American Institute of Certified Public Accountants (AICPA).

4.20   SUMMARY OF REPORTING STANDARDS

Reporting standards require that written reports will be prepared by Internal Audit in order that:

a.   Results can be clearly communicated to responsible management.

b.   Findings are less susceptible to misunderstanding.

c.   A basis for subsequent follow-up work is established to determine whether appropriate measures were taken.

POLICY HANDBOOK

AUDIT STANDARDS - REPORTING

CHAPTER 4

4.20   **SUMMARY OF REPORTING STANDARDS** (Cont...)

Four types of written reports will be used:

-     The formal report...
          For significant findings and recommendations to top
          management.

-     Priority Action Memorandum...
          Findings that require immediate attention before the
          Formal Report is ready.

-     The Letter Report...
          For minor findings that do not require controlled follow-up.

-     The Annual Report...
          Sums up audit results and provides a year long perspective
          for top management.

All reports, whenever possible, will be complete, with proper balance, and in
clear, concise language. Internal Audit will issue these reports as promptly as
possible. This makes information timely, and practical.

4.30   ADVANCE DISCUSSIONS

Audit Standards require that advance discussion be held with responsible
management as early and as often as necessary and practical. This will ensure
that by the conclusion of audit:

a.   There was ample opportunity for management to comment on
          the accuracy, completeness, fairness and significance of the
          tentative audit findings.

b.   There was advance understanding of the nature of the expected
          final audit results.

c.   Prompt corrective actions were initiated when warranted.

Advance discussion of audit findings, in the broadest sense includes all
communications, verbal or written, that relate to what the auditor has found
or is finding during an audit but which occur before the final audit report is
issued. Since these communications occur before the audit report is finalized,
in actuality they revolve around "tentative" audit findings.

AUDIT STANDARDS - REPORTING

4.30   ADVANCE DISCUSSIONS (Cont...)

It is important to note, that, although the audit process relies heavily on physical and documentary evidence, information furnished by people (testimonial evidence) constitutes important data, views, and explanations to be used by the auditor -- along with other evidence -- in reaching conclusions and recommendations.   Thus, advance discussions are a regular and integral part of the auditor's fact finding and evaluative procedures.

4.40   THE FORMAL REPORT

Purpose: This report formally concludes a scheduled audit and provides a method of presenting to senior management and the CEO significant audit conclusions that should be acted on.

Report Format: The formal report will include:

Summary-
- Audit Scope and Objectives
- Audit Opinion
- Major Audit Conclusions

Detailed Comments-
- findings, recommendations... and management's corrective action

Report Content: The basis for this report is in the working papers and record of observations of the audit staff on each assignment.

Each audit report will explain the scope and objectives of the audit and present findings accurately, completely and objectively. Wherever applicable, the elements of a deficiency finding will be described with its attributes so as, to assist the implementation of corrective action.

- Condition/Facts
- Impact/Extent
- Standards/Criteria
- Causes
- Recommendations

Primary emphasis will be placed on future improvement, rather than on criticism of the past. Any critical comments will be balanced recognizing unusual difficulties or circumstances faced by operating management.

POLICY HANDBOOK

AUDIT STANDARDS - REPORTING

CHAPTER 4

4.40   THE FORMAL REPORT (Cont...)

Reports, in order to be objective and unbiased, require proper perspective. This indicates the relative significance of the findings presented. Information needed for this 'perspective' includes:

- Data about the size and nature of the activities or programs to which the findings relate, and a carefully worded statement of the specific audit scope and objectives.

- Correct and fair descriptions of findings so as to avoid misinterpretation and misunderstanding.

- Recognition of noteworthy accomplishments, when warranted.

- Disclosure of unusual difficulties, or unique circumstances of operating management.

The formal report will include the summary judgments based on the results of audit verifications in relation to the scope. Appropriate recommendations will be set out in each report designed to correct the weaknesses, inaccuracies, or system defect.

If corrective action has been initiated and/or completed by management the report will comment on this action... if corrective action is agreed to by management the report will also reflect this commitment. If, however, there is disagreement between the auditee and the auditor regarding corrective action the report will reflect this lack of agreement.

Management's Review:

1.   A draft report is written by the auditor after audit workpapers have been reviewed and approved by the Audit Director. This draft report is considered a tentative, working document, subject to revision. As a consequence, information contained in this draft should be safeguarded against any premature disclosure and unauthorized use.

2.   Management's first review of the draft report occurs with the auditee or operating manager and the auditor. The purpose of this meeting is twofold: to agree on the written findings and proposed corrective action. It is not intended to be a briefing session but rather a meeting to reach agreement... what needs to be implemented to correct the problem.

POLICY HANDBOOK

AUDIT STANDARDS - REPORTING

CHAPTER 4

4.40   THE FORMAL REPORT (Cont...)

If during the audit, corrective action has been initiated and/or completed by the auditee, the findings will indicate this action. If, however, action has not been implemented, the auditee is expected to be prepared to fully discuss and commit to correcting the deficiency. The auditor will update the draft report to reflect the auditee's plan of action.

3.   The vice president in charge of the audited area will receive this draft report after it has been updated with the auditee's comments and plan of action. The issuance of this draft report to senior management will be made with the knowledge of the Vice-President, Management Resources.

4.   The draft report is the basis for an exit conference with the auditee's vice-president. This is senior management's opportunity to comment on the contents of the report as well as to discuss and/or resolve any problem with the auditee's plan of action. Attendees at this meeting may include all responsible persons - operating and senior management - pertinent to the audit under review.

5.   Exit conferences should occur within a reasonable time frame. However, if unreasonable delays are encountered the audit report will be issued. If this should occur, an explanation will be included in the report.

6.   The formal report will normally be issued to the Chief Executive Officer (CEO) after it has been reviewed by appropriate senior management. The distribution will include GHC's external auditors.

7.   Issuance of the final, formal report will not be contingent upon receiving written responses from management. However, the auditee is expected to provide Internal Audit with written confirmation regarding action completed or their plan of action within 30 days of issuing the report to the CEO.

Follow-up On Audit Recommendations:

It is the responsibility of senior management to see that corrective action is taken on deficient conditions reported by Internal Audit. Internal Audit will review and report on the actions taken and determine their effectiveness.

If the auditee's corrective action is not completed within the 'confirmation period' (first 30 days) a status report from the auditee is expected until the action is completed. Internal Audit will determine the frequency of these status reports.

POLICY HANDBOOK
AUDIT STANDARDS - REPORTING
CHAPTER 4

4.40   THE FORMAL REPORT (Cont...)

A status report questionnaire will be sent to the auditee from Internal Audit. If the reply from the auditee is not returned promptly a second notification will include the auditee's vice-president along with a copy to the Vice-President, Management Resources.

Internal Audit will provide the CEO with a status update regarding all outstanding items, i.e., all proposed and uncompleted corrective action. Where it is determined by Internal Audit that management's action is also untimely or deficient this condition will be included in the update...it will also be referred to the Vice-President, Management Resources for consideration.

4.50   PRIORITY ACTION MEMORANDUM (PAMs):

Purpose: PAMs will be used by Internal Audit to advise senior management and the CEO of very serious findings/exposures requiring prompt attention and resolution.

Report Format and Content: PAMs will be short. Minimal information may be provided so as to enable immediate attention by top management. Primary emphasis will be to obtain timely corrective action without procedural delay.

Audit Responsibility: It is the responsibility of the Director of Internal Audit to determine the circumstances requiring a PAM; i.e., the nature of the finding - its magnitude, complexity and degree of exposure. The issuance of a PAM will be made with the knowledge and agreement of the Vice-President, Management Resources.

Management's Review:

1.   PAMs will be issued to the appropriate vice-president and CEO.

2.   The Director of Internal Audit will meet immediately with the respective vice-president to discuss the problem and its resolution. A meeting with the CEO will occur subsequently. However, if a delay is encountered with the vice-president the PAM will be presented to the CEO without the benefit of additional input and/or information.

POLICY HANDBOOK
AUDIT STANDARDS - REPORTING
CHAPTER 4

4.60   THE LETTER REPORT

Purpose: This report will be used to communicate minor findings which require correction but do not affect the accomplishment of significant goals and objectives.

Report Format and Content: This minor report is directed to the operating manager who can take action but it does not require a formal, written response.   In this way, the follow-up process is not overburdened with monitoring items of lessor significance.

4.70   THE ANNUAL REPORT

Purpose: This report will sum up individual audit efforts and provide a yearly overview of audit accomplishments, activities and their total significance.

Report Content: The report will normally include the following supporting data:

- Comparison of work programmed with work accomplished

- Number of areas covered

- Number of reports issued

- Number of communications to management

- Cost of operating the auditing department

- Amounts of estimated recoveries and savings compared to actual, if applicable

POLICY HANDBOOK

SUPPLEMENTAL COMPUTER RELATED STANDARDS

CHAPTER 5

5.00   INTRODUCTION

When a system to be audited is operated by or involves the use of a computer, GHC supplemental standards for auditing computer-based systems provide the basic policy guidance for this audit work. These computer auditing standards concern audit work in three major computer-related areas:

    ...   design and development of computer-based systems,

    ...   general controls in computer-based systems, and

    ...   application controls in computer-based systems.

POLICY HANDBOOK

SUPPLEMENTAL COMPUTER RELATED STANDARDS

CHAPTER 5

5.10   **STANDARD FOR INTERNAL AUDIT'S ROLE DURING SYSTEMS DESIGN AND DEVELOPMENT**

"The auditor will actively participate in reviewing the design and development of new data processing systems or applications, and/or any significant modification as a normal part of the audit function."

The scope of auditing within computerized systems includes coverage of the design and development of significant new systems and any planned modifications to these systems. These computerized systems include those systems and operations which have a major role in management operations, expenditures and/or program accomplishments.

5.10.10   Objectives of First Supplemental Standard

The objectives of Internal Audit's role during system design and development are to assure senior management that systems/applications:

      ...   faithfully carry out the policies operating management has prescribed for the system;

      ...   provide the controls and audit trails needed for management, auditor and operational review;

      ...   include controls necessary to protect against loss or serious error;

      ...   are efficient and economical in operation;

      ...   conform with applicable legal, privacy and budgetary considerations; and

      ...   are documented in a manner that will provide the understanding of the system required for appropriate maintenance and auditing.

5.10.11   Management Policies

The first objective places upon the auditor the responsibility for determining whether the design for the planned EDP system reflects management's requirements. The audit coverage will include:

POLICY HANDBOOK
SUPPLEMENTAL COMPUTER RELATED STANDARDS
CHAPTER 5

5.10.11   **Management Policies** (Cont...)

    ...   ascertaining that the appropriate approval process is being
            followed including the approval of system design by data
            processing management, user groups and others whose data
            and reports may be affected;

    ...   reviewing security provisions to protect data and programs
            against unauthorized access and modification; and

    ...   determining whether appropriate management and computer
            controls are in place.

Importance is placed on the auditor's retention of independence during the
system design and development cycle. Independence is enhanced by reporting
the review results to top management for resolution of adverse findings.

5.10.12   Audit Trail

This feature is essential in both financial and non-financial systems in order to
determine the completeness and reliability of the system output.

In the development of EDP systems it is technically possible to produce a
system with such poor controls features that it cannot be audited. The
adverse effect of this situation is that neither the system user nor the auditor
can place reliance on the integrity of the processing or the output. Reviews
of audit trail requirements provide management with additional assurance
that auditable and controlled systems will be produced.

5.10.13   Controls

The third objective stresses that designed EDP systems include control
mechanisms to protect against loss and serious error. Manual and automatic
control interfaces should be included in this audit coverage.

This review includes: identifying areas in the system where controls are
needed, determining the absence or presence of controls, and evaluating
through testing the adequacy of manual and built-in controls to protect
against error and/or loss.

POLICY HANDBOOK

SUPPLEMENTAL COMPUTER RELATED STANDARDS

CHAPTER 5

5.10.14   Efficiency and Economy

The fourth objective emphasizes that computer systems will be efficient and economical in operation. Satisfying this objective requires a review for the adequacy of:

      ...   system objectives to meet management needs;

      ...   the feasibility study and evaluation of alternative designs; and

      ...   cost benefit analysis attributing specific costs and benefits to alternative system designs.

5.10.15   Legal Requirements

The fifth objective assures that computer systems will be in conformance with applicable privacy and/or legal requirements.

5.10.16   Documentation

The sixth objective involves determining that proposed EDP systems are documented to provide sufficient information in maintaining and auditing the system.

This objective also involves determining whether management policy provides for sufficient testing to assure that reliance can be placed on the system before its implementation into production.

5.20   STANDARD FOR GENERAL EDP CONTROLS

"The auditor shall review general controls in data processing systems to determine that (a) controls have been designed according to management directions and legal requirements, and (b) such controls are operating effectively to provide reliability of, and security over, data being processed."

The accuracy and completeness of computer processing depends on general EDP controls within the computer facility and all operating and communications systems. These general controls are pervasive controls. Failure of any of these controls can affect all applications and their associated data.

POLICY HANDBOOK
SUPPLEMENTAL COMPUTER RELATED STANDARDS
CHAPTER 5

5.20.10   Objectives of Second Supplemental Standard

The objectives of Internal Audit's role in evaluating general EDP controls are to assure that:

...   the plan of organization and operation of the EDP activity at GHC provide for controlled delegation of authority and the proper assignment of responsibilities.

...   standards and procedures for documenting, reviewing, testing and approving system or program changes exist and are used effectively.

...   hardware, software and communications systems are in place and operating properly.

...   access to equipment and data files is closely controlled and secure.

...   data and procedural controls affecting overall EDP operations reflect adequate contingency planning.

5.20.11   Plan of Organization and Operation of EDP Activity

The first objective in evaluating general EDP controls is to ascertain that the organizational controls include the necessary levels of authority and responsibility to efficiently and effectively establish objectives.

An audit should include a review of the:

...   organization,

...   delegation of authority,

...   assigned responsibilities.

The objective is to determine whether functional lines of authority and assignment of responsibilities are designated to provide separation of duties and functions needed for a strong level of internal control.

POLICY HANDBOOK
SUPPLEMENTAL COMPUTER RELATED STANDARDS
CHAPTER 5

5.20.12   Documentation, Review, Testing and Approval of Changes

The auditor should review the procedures that are used to control and document changes to operating, application, and communication systems.

The audit of these areas should include a review of:

...   documentation to determine if it is current and up to industry and department standards,

...   testing procedures to insure that all software and hardware changes are adequately tested,

...   the approval process for all changes to determine that changes are approved by appropriate authority.

5.20.13   Hardware, Operating System and Communication Controls

The auditor's review of controls in the areas of hardware, operating systems and communications is critical.   A breakdown of these areas will affect all computer processing and data integrity.

The review should include the determination that:

...   manufacturer's hardware controls are in place and operating properly,

...   the operating system software, including communications software, is maintained in a tightly controlled environment.

...   all access and changes to systems software are closely controlled and thoroughly documented.

5.20.14   Access to Equipment and Data Files

Access to computer facilities, equipment and data files should be closely controlled.   The auditor should review security used to control access.   Audit coverage in this area would include determinations of whether:

...   access to computer hardware, including terminals, is limited to authorized personnel,

POLICY HANDBOOK

SUPPLEMENTAL COMPUTER RELATED STANDARDS

CHAPTER 5

5.20.14   **Access to Equipment and Data Files** (Cont...)

...   computer equipment is adequately protected against fire, flood, water damage or other natural disasters,

...   off-site storage of data and programs is adequate,

...   access to data and programs is properly controlled.

5.20.15   Other Data and Procedural Controls

Other types of administrative, procedural controls are necessary to ensure continued and adequate operation of data processing.   A review of contingency plans, which are developed for the continued processing of critical applications, will be made. This type of review should cover elements of good disaster planning - provisions for back-up facilities, communications, hardware, software, personnel and other considerations for both data processors and users.

5.30   STANDARD FOR APPLICATION CONTROLS IN COMPUTER-BASED SYSTEMS

"The auditor shall review application controls of installed data processing applications to assess their reliability in the recording, processing and reporting of data in a timely, accurate and complete manner."

EDP audits include consideration of application controls to see that the recording of data responds to management's needs for current, useful and accurate information.

5.30.10   Objectives of Third Supplemental Standard

The objectives of auditing an application system are to determine that internal controls within the computerized system are adequate to provide assurances that data are recorded, processed and reported accurately, timely, and in compliance with management's directives.

POLICY HANDBOOK

SUPPLEMENTAL COMPUTER RELATED STANDARDS

CHAPTER 5

5.30.10   Objectives of Third Supplemental Standard (Cont...)

An audit of an application would review and test:

    ...   documentation;

    ...   internal control weaknesses;

    ...   transaction origination controls;

    ...   computer processing controls;

    ...   data storage and retrieval controls; and

    ...   output processing controls.

5.30.11   Documentation of Application Systems

These audits will ensure that statements of objective, flowcharts, input forms, screen descriptions, record and database formats, and audit trails properly relate to the operating application; and that, administrative and accounting control procedures are in effect. The results of acceptance testing and post-installation reviews conducted by data processors, users or internal auditors should be reviewed for leads to design or control features not in conformity with specifications.

5.30.12   Testing for Control Weaknesses

This type of audit probes installed computer system/applications for weaknesses in internal controls.   Tests should be conducted of major (essential) controls which a preliminary survey indicates may be weak or inoperative.   Control tests are required to verify that designed internal control features are actually in place and effective in assuring complete and accurate data processing.

Tests may encompass six phases of application processing - transaction origination, data entry, data communications, computer processing, data storage/retrieval and output processing.

POLICY HANDBOOK

SUPPLEMENTAL COMPUTER RELATED STANDARDS

CHAPTER 5

5.30.12   Testing for Control Weaknesses (Cont...)

In performing the survey and tests, auditors should keep in mind that system/applications may not include all designed controls or operate in accordance with approved specifications. Also, the possibility of fraud or error always exists. Though fraud and error detection are not the primary objectives of testing controls in computerized systems, weak internal controls may lead to fraud or error.

5.30.13   Testing Transaction Origination Controls

Transaction origination controls govern the manual preparation and processing of transactions prior to data entry. They include control features over source documents that become inputs to the computer system and encompass source document authorization, document preparation for data entry, document retention and control, error handling and batch controls.

Testing of transaction origination controls should focus on procedures to assure:

    ...   proper authorization of source documents and identification of unauthorized documents;

    ...   proper and timely preparation for data entry;

    ...   control of document flow between involved departments;

    ...   detection of errors, their correction and timely re-entry into the system; and

    ...   proper retention of source documents to provide audit trails and back-up for recovering information lost or destroyed.

5.30.14   Testing Transaction Entry Controls

Application controls relate to batch data entry and terminal (online) entry operations, generally involving manual and automated procedures. They include controls over keypunching and verifying, online data entry, computer validation of input, and error correction.

The audit should include sufficient testing of data entry controls to establish their adequacy in allowing only complete, accurate and authorized data to

POLICY HANDBOOK

SUPPLEMENTAL COMPUTER RELATED STANDARDS

CHAPTER 5

5.30.14   **Testing Transaction Entry Controls** (Cont...)

enter into computer processing. The review should test the following control features:

> ...   logging of data received for data entry;

> ...   method used to convert data into machine readable formats;

> ...   validation of the completeness of data entered into the computer and identification of errors;

> ...   physical security controlling access to online input devices;

> ...   password security limiting operation of online devices to authorized operators; and

> ...   correction of errors and the timely re-entry of corrected data.

These controls ensure that data flow between remote terminal locations and processing centers is complete and accurate; that messages are accounted for and protected; and that errors are reported and corrected. The purpose of audit is to:

> ...   check the adequacy of physical safeguards limiting access to computer terminals;

> ...   test the physical and software controls that permit only authorized personnel to use remote terminals;

> ...   review hardware and software controls governing message transmissions between terminals and receiving hardware/software; and

> ...   test controls at the computer center governing receipt and accounting for message traffic.

The audit should also include reviewing error logs and reports. These can provide leads to problems in the communications network. Also, it should be determined whether corrective action has been taken.

POLICY HANDBOOK

SUPPLEMENTAL COMPUTER RELATED STANDARDS

CHAPTER 5

5.30.15   Testing Computer Processing Controls

Automated controls in computer applications programs perform specific processing functions. An audit should include tests to determine if these control are adequate in:

... preventing errors and omissions in data within and between computer programs and systems;

... preventing loss of data in event of disruption of processing or error conditions;

... ensuring accuracy of mathematical computations;

... governing operator intervention through the computer console;

... preventing accidental or unauthorized use of application programs;

... identifying and reporting errors;

... providing audit trails; and

... controlling automatically generated transactions to prevent errors or unauthorized/illegal transactions.

Testing computer processing controls entails auditing through the computer using advanced auditing techniques.

5.30.16   Testing Data Storage and Retrieval Controls

These controls ensure the accuracy, completeness and security of master files maintained for the system/application under review. They include procedures over the updating of master files, cut off of fiscal year end data, data security and error handling.

The thrust of audit testing in this control area are to:

... verify the accuracy of master record data through confirmation of totals or other data to records outside data processing;

POLICY HANDBOOK

SUPPLEMENTAL COMPUTER RELATED STANDARDS

CHAPTER 5

5.30.16   Testing Data Storage and Retrieval Controls (Cont...)

...   evaluate procedures for accurately updating master records;

...   determine the adequacy of security measures in effect for the storage of master files and their movement between the tape library and computer site;

...   verify the maintenance and usability of back-up files for recovery in event of the destruction of master files; and

...   determine the adequacy of procedures for identifying and correcting errors.

5.30.17   Testing Output Processing Controls

Properly designed output controls can assure the accuracy and completeness of data processing. They include methods for balancing/reconciling output to input; procedures for ensuring the delivery of computer output to the proper user at the required time; controls to retain output in accordance with legal, accounting and administrative requirements; and methods for identifying and correcting errors.

Output controls should be tested to the extent necessary to establish whether designed controls are actually in effect and are accurate. The audit should check output reports to verify the mathematical accuracy of displayed data, relate the output to its input and verify that distribution was made on a timely basis to only authorized users. The actual retention of output should also be compared against established retention schedules. In addition, procedures for routine reconciliation of output to input should be evaluated as well as procedures for error reporting and correcting. Computer matches to screen and analyze data from two or more computer files of information may be used to determine errors, waste, and/or fraud.

In audits where checks or other negotiable documents are automatically produced by the computer, emphasis should be placed on determining the adequacy of controls over these sensitive computer outputs. The audit should probe established controls over the handling, processing, signing and distributing of these computer products.

STANDARDS
FOR THE PROFESSIONAL PRACTICE
OF INTERNAL AUDITING

430   Communicating Results

Internal Auditors should report the results of their audit work.

1.   A signed, written report should be used after the audit examination as completed. Interim reports may be written or oral and may be transmitted formally or informally.

2.   The internal auditor should discuss conclusions and recommendations at appropriate levels of management before issuing final written reports.

3.   Reports should be objective, clear, concise, constructive, and timely.

4.   Reports should present the purpose, scope, and results of the audit; and, where appropriate, reports should contain an expression of the auditor's opinion.

5.   Reports may include recommendations for potential improvements and acknowledge satisfactory performance and corrective action.

6.   The auditee's views about audit conclusions or recommendations may be included in the audit report.

7.   The director of internal auditing or designee should review and approve the final audit report before issuance and should decide to whom the report will be distributed.

The Institute of Internal Auditors, Inc.
Adopted 1978

APPENDIX II

GENERALLY ACCEPTED AUDITING STANDARDS
AICPA Professional Standards

.01   Auditing standards differ from auditing procedures in that "procedures" relate to acts to be performed, whereas "standards" deal with measures of the quality of the performance of those acts and objectives to be attained by the use of the procedures undertaken.   Auditing standards as distinct from auditing procedures concern themselves not only with the auditor's professional qualities but also with the judgment exercised by him in the performance of his examination and his report.

.02   The generally accepted auditing standards as approved and adopted by the membership of the American Institute of Certified Public Accountants are as follows:

General Standards

1.   The examination is to be performed by a person or persons having adequate technical training and proficiency as an auditor.

2.   In all matters relating to the assignment, an independence in mental attitude is to be maintained by the auditor or auditors.

3.   Due professional care is to be exercised in the performance of the examination and the preparation of the report.

Standards of Field Work

1.   The work is to be adequately planned and assistants, if any, are to be properly supervised.

2.   There is to be proper study and evaluation of the existing internal control as a basis for reliance thereon and for the determination of the resultant extent of the tests to which auditing procedures are to be restricted.

3.   Sufficient competent evidential matter is to be obtained through inspection, observation, inquiries, and confirmations to afford a reasonable basis for an opinion regarding the financial statements under examination.

Standards of Reporting

1.   The report shall state whether the financial statement are presented in accordance with generally accepted accounting principles.

Standards of Reporting (Cont..)

2. The report shall state whether the financial statement are presented in accordance with generally accepted accounting principles.

3. Informative disclosures in the financial statements are to be regarded as reasonably adequate unless otherwise stated in the report.

4. The report shall either contain an expression of opinion regarding the financial statements, taken as a whole, or an assertion to the effect that an opinion cannot be expressed. When an overall opinion cannot be expressed, the reasons therefor should be stated. In all cases where an auditor's name is associated with financial statement, the report should contain a clear-cut indication of the character of the auditor's examination, if any, and the degree of responsibility he is taking.

APPENDIX III

THE EFFECT OF EDP ON THE AUDITOR'S STUDY
AND EVALUATION OF INTERNAL CONTROL*

Issue date,
unless otherwise
indicated:
December, 1974

Introduction

.01   Section 320, "The Auditor's Study and Evaluation of Internal Control,"
defines internal control in terms of administrative control and accounting
co rol. That section also sets forth the basic concepts of accounting control
and concludes that accounting control is within the scope of the study and
evaluation of internal control contemplated be generally accepted auditing
standards, while administrative control is not.

.02   Section 320.33 discusses methods of data processing as follows:

Since the definition and related basic concepts of accounting control
are expressed in terms of objectives, they are independent of the
method of data processing used; consequently, they apply equally to
manual, mechanical, and electronic data processing systems.
However, the organization and procedures required to accomplish
those objectives may be influenced by the method of data processing
used.

Because the method of data processing used may influence the organization
and procedures employed by an entity to accomplish the objectives of
accounting control, it may also influence the procedures employed by an
auditor in his study and evaluation of accounting control to determine the
nature, timing, and extent of audit procedures to be applied in his examination
of financial statements.

.03   A data processing system may be wholly manual or may include a
combination of manual activities, mechanical activities, and electronic data
processing (EDP) activities. EDP applications vary considerably, from routine
applications that process a small payroll to complex, integrated applications
that process accounting, production, marketing, and administrative information simultaneously. In some data processing systems, accounting control
procedures are performed by people in one or more departments. In EDP
systems, many or even most of these control procedures may be performed by
the EDP process itself. When EDP is used in significant accounting
applications, the auditor should consider the EDP activity in his study and
evaluation of accounting control. This is true whether the use of EDP in
accounting applications is limited or extensive and whether the EDP facilities
are operated under the direction of the auditor's client or third party.

*AICPA Professional Standards

.04   The first general auditing standard is as follows: "The examination is to be performed by a person or persons having adequate technical training and proficiency as an auditor." If a client uses EDP in its accounting system, whether the application is simple or complex, the auditor needs to understand the entire system sufficiently to enable him to identify and evaluate its essential accounting control features. Situations involving the more complex EDP applications ordinarily will require that the auditor apply specialized expertise in EDP in the performance of the necessary audit procedures.

.05   This section describes the effects of the use of EDP on the various characteristics of accounting control and on an auditor's study and evaluation thereof. It is intended to be read in conjuction with section 320. The concepts in this Statement are expressed in general terms. An auditor likely will need to refer to other sources of information to apply the concepts in particular audit situations. Those sources include continuing education courses, data processing manuals, current textbooks, and current professional literature.

EDP Account Control Procedures

.06   Some EDP accounting control procedures relate to all EDP activities (general controls) and some relate to a specific accounting task, such as preparation of account listings or payrolls (application controls).

.07   General controls comprise (a) the plan of organization and operation of the EDP activity, (b) the procedures for documenting, reviewing, testing and approving systems or programs and changes thereto, (c) controls built into the equipment by the manufacturer (commonly referred to as "hardware controls"), (d) controls over access to equipment and data files, and (e) other data and procedural controls affecting overall EDP operations. Weaknesses in general controls often have pervasive effects. When general controls are weak or absent, the auditor should consider the effect of such weakness or absence in the evaluation of application controls.

.08   Application controls relate to specific tasks performed by EDP. Their function is to provide reasonable assurance that the recording, processing, and reporting of data are properly performed. There is considerable choice in the particular procedures and records used to effect application controls. Application controls often are categorized as "input controls," processing controls," and "output controls."

      a.   Input controls are designed to provide reasonable assurance that data received for processing by EDP have been properly authorized, converted into machine sensible form and identified, and that data (including data transmitted over communication lines) have not been lost, suppressed, added, duplicated, or otherwise improperly changed. Input controls include controls that relate to rejection, correction, and resubmission of data that were initially incorrect.

b.   Processing controls are designed to provide reasonable assurance that electronic data processing has been performed as intended for the particular application; i.e., that all transactions are processed as authorized, that no authorized transactions are omitted, and that no unauthorized transactions are added.

c.   Output controls are designed to assure the accuracy of the processing result (such as account listings or displays, reports, magnetic files, invoices, or disbursement checks) and to assure that only authorized personnel receive the output.

.09   EDP accounting control procedures may be performed within an EDP organization, a user department, or a separate control group. The department or unit in which accounting control procedures are performed is less significant than the performance of the procedures by persons having no incompatible functions for accounting control purposes and the effectiveness of the procedures.

The Effects of EDP on the Characteristics of Accounting Control

.10   The objectives and the essential characteristics of accounting control do not change with the method of data processing. However, organization and control procedures used in electronic data processing may differ from those used in manual or mechanical data processing. For example, electronic data processing of sales, billings, and accounts receivable may perform the ancillary function of verifying invoice totals and extensions, a control that usually is established in manual data processing through independent clerical calculations. Further, in some EDP systems (such as one using direct terminal input as the basic source of data to be processed in a payroll, cost accounting, or inventory control application) control functions that otherwise would be performed by several individuals and departments may be concentrated within the EDP activity. Paragraphs .11 through .23 describe the effects of EDP on the essential characteristics of accounting control.

Segregation of Functions

.11   As set forth in section 320.36, incompatible functions for accounting control purposes are those that place any person in a position both to perpetrate and to conceal errors or irregularities in the normal course of his duties. Many EDP systems not only process accounting data but also include procedures for detecting errors and irregularities and for providing specific authorization for certain kinds of transactions. Since the procedures may be combined, incompatible functions may be more likely to be combined in an EDP activity than in a manual activity.

Segregation of Functions (Cont...)

.12 Frequently, functions that would be considered incompatible if performed by a single individual in a manual activity are performed through the use of an EDP program or series of programs. A person having the opportunity to make unapproved changes to any such programs performs incompatible functions in relation to the EDP activity. For example, a program for an accounts-payable application may have been designed to process for payment a vendor's invoice only if accompanied by a purchase-order record agreeing with the invoice as to prices and quantities and a receiving record indicating receipt of the goods or services. In the absence of adequate control over program changes, an unapproved revision might change the application so that unsubstantiated payments could be made to vendors.

.13 EDP data files frequently are basic records of an accounting system. They cannot be read or changed without the use of EDP, but they can be changed through the use of EDP without visible evidence that a change has occurred. A person in a position to make unapproved changes in EDP data files performs incompatible functions. In the example of the accounts-payable application in the preceding paragraph, an individual who could make unapproved changes in the files containing purchase orders and receiving reports might be able to add spurious records purporting to represent purchase orders and receiving reports to the files, thereby causing the program to process for payment unapproved vendor invoices.

.14 Supervisory programs are used in some EDP systems to perform generalized functions for more than one application program. Supervisory programs include (a) "operating systems," which control EDP equipment that may process one or more application programs at a given time and (b) "data management systems," which perform standardized data handling functions for one or more application programs. An individual who can make unapproved changes in supervisory programs has opportunities to initiate unauthorized transactions that are like those of a person who can make unapproved changes in application programs or data files; he therefore performs incompatible functions.

.15 Paragraphs .11 through .14 discuss incompatible functions related to matters such as assignment of duties, changes in programs, maintenance of data files, and operating or data management systems. If individuals involved perform incompatible functions, compensating controls may be applied. For example, a plan of organization and operation may contain controls and provisions for effective supervision and rotation of personnel. Also, user departments or other control groups may establish independent document counts or totals of significant data fields. Compensating controls frequently are supplemented by internal audit procedures.

Execution of Transactions

.16 The extent to which EDP is used to execute steps in a transaction cycle varies. For example, EDP may be used in an accounting application for reordering materials: (a) to determine items to be ordered and prepare the

Execution of Transactions (Cont...)

purchase orders, (b) to identify items that require replenishment and prepare a notification list for use by purchasing department personnel, or (c) to prepare inventory listing for review by purchasing department personnel.

.17   To the extent that EDP is used to execute steps in a transaction cycle, the EDP application program usually includes accounting control procedures designed to assure that the steps are executed in conformity with specific or general authorizations issued by persons (including, in advanced systems, customers or other persons not employed by the entity) acting within the scope of their authority. Those procedures might include checks to recognize data that fall outside predetermined limits and tests for overall reasonableness.

Recording of Transactions

.18   Account control is concerned with recording of transactions at the amounts and in the accounting periods in which they were executed and with their classification in appropriate accounts. The use of EDP to process or initiate and record transactions may affect the source and extent of possible errors.

.19   To be usable in EDP, data are converted into machine-sensible form. The initial recording of the transactions or the initiation of transactions by the processing of previously recorded data may introduce errors that could affect balances and reports unless data input is properly controlled. Procedures of various types are used to maintain accounting control over data conversion. Some are manual, some are an integral part of the EDP program, and some are built into the EDP equipment by the manufacturer.

.20   The use of EDP often provides an opportunity to improve accounting control relating to the recording of transactions. For example, EDP equipment is not subject to errors caused by fatigue or carelessness. It processes and records like transactions in a like manner. It may be programmed to detect certain types of invalid or unusual transactions. The procedures for these purposes may be more comprehensive, effective, and efficient than manual control procedures having the same objectives. On the other hand, a transaction may be processed incorrectly by EDP if the EDP program does not provide for the particular set of relevant circumstances, whereas the same transaction might be questioned in a manual system.

.21   The effectiveness of accounting control over the recording of transaction by EDP depends on both   (a) the functioning of the EDP procedures that record the transactions and produce the output (such as account listings or displays, summaries, magnetic files, and exception reports) and (b) the follow-up or other actions of users of the output. For example, an EDP program might reject from further processing invoices with improperly coded customer numbers.

Recording of Transactions (Cont...)

However, if users who receive exception reports on those items do not correct the customer numbers and resubmit the invoices for processing, accounts receivable and sales will be understated.

Access to Assets

.22   EDP personnel have access to assets if the EDP activity includes the preparation or processing of documents that lead to the use or disposition of the assets. EDP personnel have direct access to cash, for example, if the EDP activity includes the preparation and signing of disbursement checks. Sometimes access by EDP personnel to assets may not be readily apparent because the access is indirect. For example, EDP may generate payment orders authorizing issuance of checks, shipping orders authorizing release of inventory, or transfer orders authorizing release or customer-owned securities. Controls such as those discussed in paragraph .15 should be established to minimize the possibility of unauthorized access to assets by EDP personnel.

Comparison of Recorded Accountability with Assets

.23   EDP frequently is used to compare recorded accountability with assets. For example, EDP may summarize physical counts of inventories or securities and compare the recorded quantities with the summarized counts. If EDP is so used, conditions under which errors or irregularities may occur should be considered. For example, there may be opportunities to overstate physical counts, insert fictitious physical counts, or suppress the printout of differences. Many of the considerations described in paragraphs .18 through .21 may also apply.

Review of the System

.24   An auditor's review of a client's system of accounting control should encompass all significant and relevant manual, mechanical, and EDP activities and the interrelationship between EDP and user departments. The review should comprehend both the control procedures related to transactions from origination or source to recording in the accounting records and the control procedures related to recorded accountability for assets. The objectives of the auditor's review of accounting control within EDP are similar to those for manual and mechanical processing. The review is an information-gathering process that depends on knowledgeable inquiries directed to client personnel, observation of job assignments and operating procedures, and reference to available documentation related to accounting control.

Review of the System (Cont...)

.25   The preliminary phase of an auditor's review should be designed to provide an understanding of the flow of transactions through the accounting system, the extent to which EDP is used in each significant accounting application, and the basic structure of accounting control. During the preliminary phase, the auditor may identify some of the specified accounting control procedures relating to each application and may become aware of apparent material weaknesses in the procedures. The auditor's preliminary understanding ordinarily is obtained by inquiry, but it also may be obtained by observing client personnel and reviewing documentation. Such preliminary understanding of EDP procedures normally relates to the general controls and application controls discussed in paragraphs .06 through .09.

.26   After completing the preliminary phase of his review as described in paragraph .25, for each significant accounting application the auditor should be in a position to assess the significance of accounting control within EDP in relation to the entire system of accounting control and therefore to determine the extent of his review of EDP accounting control.

      a.   The auditor may conclude that accounting control procedures within the EDP portions of the application or applications appear to provide a basis for reliance thereon and for restricting the extent of his substantive tests. In that event, unless the auditor chose to follow the procedures described in paragraph .26c, he would complete his review of the EDP accounting control procedures, perform related tests of compliance, and evaluate the control procedures to determine the extent of his reliance thereon and the extent to which substantive tests may be restricted.

      b.   The auditor may conclude that there are weaknesses in accounting control procedures in the EDP portions of the application or applications sufficient to preclude his reliance on such procedures. In that event, he would discontinue his review on those EDP accounting control procedures and forgo performing compliance tests related to those procedures; he would not be able to rely on those EDP accounting control procedures. The auditor would assess the potential impact on the financial statements he is examining of such weaknesses as have come to his attention, and would accomplish his audit objectives by other means.

      c.   The auditor may decide not to extent his preliminary review and not to perform tests of compliance related to accounting control procedures (either in general or as to certain procedures) within the EDP portions of the application or applications even though he concludes that the controls appear adequate. In that event, he would be able to rely on those EDP accounting control procedures. Situations of this type could be those in which –

Review of System (Cont...)

    (1)   The auditor concludes that the audit effort required to complete his review and test compliance would exceed the reduction in effort that could be achieved by reliance upon the EDP accounting controls.

    (2)   The auditor concludes that certain EDP accounting control procedures are redundant because other accounting control procedures are in existence.

Tests of Compliance

.27   The purpose of tests of compliance is to provide reasonable assurance that accounting control procedures are being applied as prescribed. Tests of compliance are concerned primarily with the questions: (a) Were the necessary procedures performed? (b) How were they performed? (c) By whom were they performed?

.28   Some accounting control procedures within the EDP activity leave visible evidence indicating that the procedures were performed. An example of such evidence is a file documenting (a) program changes for each EDP application and (b) approval of the changes. Other example are EDP-generated error listings and exception reports.

.29   Some accounting control procedures within the EDP activity, especially those in programs that are designed to detect erroneous or invalid data, leave no visible evidence indicating that the procedures were performed. Then, the auditor should test these controls by reviewing transactions submitted for processing to determine that no transactions tested have unacceptable conditions or that unacceptable conditions present were reported and appropriately resolved. The review may be done manually if conditions permit, or the auditor may be able or find it necessary to use EDP to detect unacceptable conditions, either by using his own independent programs or by using copies of the client's programs that the auditor had independently determined to be adequate for his purposes. An alternative approach to testing compliance with accounting control procedures in computer programs is to review and test the programs and then to perform tests to provide assurance that the tested programs actually were used for processing. However, the auditor should be aware that this approach can be used only when effective controls exist over access and changes to programs used for processing.

.30   Some accounting control procedures within the EDP activity leave neither visible nor machine-readable evidence. For example, one of the major characteristics of accounting control is the proper segregation of functions. Evidence that such accounting control procedures are functioning is obtained by observing client personnel and making corroborative inquiries.

Evaluation of the System

.31   Evaluation of the EDP aspects of a system of accounting control is
not different conceptually from the evaluation of other aspects of the system
and should be an integral part of the auditor's evaluation of the system.
Accounting control procedures performed both within the EDP activity and by
user departments influence the effectiveness of the system and should be
considered together by the auditor. The effects of the auditor's evaluation on
the extent of his other auditing procedures are described in section 320.69-75.

GAO STANDARDS FOR COMPUTER AUDITING

The transition from manual to electronic data processing necessitates a revision of traditional audit approaches. The complexity and scope of such systems requires that the auditor give greater attention to both the system processing the data and the data itself. If the system is reasonably secure and adequately controlled, the auditor can rely on the data processed and reported.

AUDIT OBJECTIVES

The goals of an EDP application audit are to:
- Review general controls in data processing systems to determine whether the controls have been designed according to management direction and known legal requirements and whether the controls are operating effectively to provide reliability of, and security over, the data being processed.

- Review application controls of installed data processing applications on which the auditor is relying to assess their reliability in processing data in a timely, accurate, and complete manner.

In addition to reviewing general and application controls, the auditor should become involved in the design and development of new data processing system or applications and significant modifications to existing systems.

It is possible that a data processing system may have such poor controls that neither the manager nor the auditor can rely on its integrity. The auditor's review during the design and development of systems is crucial if management is to have reasonable assurance that auditable and properly controlled systems are being developed. Although compliance with this objective may not always be feasible-audit organizations may not have the resources or staff skills to carry out such a review-their involvement with systems development should be an auditing goal.

REVIEW OF GENERAL CONTROLS

The auditor should distinguish between general and application controls. General controls are usually applicable to the majority of data processing carried out with an installation; application controls may vary among applications and are therefore reviewed on an individual basis. The auditor must consider the effectiveness of the general controls on the system while reviewing individual controls.

Organizational Controls

Authority and responsibility must be delegated in such a manner that the organizational objectives can be met efficiently and effectively. The auditor should review the organization's delegation of authority, assignment of responsibilities, and separation of duties. The goal is to determine whether lines of authority are designed to meet the organization's objectives and whether the separation of duties provide for strong internal control. For example, whenever feasible, there should be a separation of duties among program and systems development functions, computer operations, controls over data input, and the control groups that maintain application controls. The total system must be considered.

In reviewing separation of duties, the auditor should evaluate the control strengths and report on weaknesses resulting from inadequate separation. Policies of periodic rotation of employees and mandatory vacation scheduling may help management maintain adequate separation of duties. The auditor should determine whether such policies are being followed.

Physical Facilities, Personnel, and Security

Adequate physical facilities and other resources (e.g., sufficently trained personnel and supplies) are necessary for the organization to meet its data processing objectives. The auditor should determine whether the organization has the resources to meet its needs.

Personnel management, including supervision, motivation, and professional development, is integral to successful data processing. The auditor should evaluate management policies and practices to ascertain whether the necessary policies exist and determine whether they are properly followed. For example, because of rapid changes in computer technology, an organization's personnel management department, in conjunction with the data processing staff, need to develop an education and training program. This program should keep employees up to date on current developments so that they may perform their duties most efficiently and economically and be able to use new methods whenever they are demonstrably cost effective. Inadequate DP personnel training and development programs can hinder accomplishment of the organization's goals.

The auditor should determine whether security provisions for computer hardware, programs, data files, data transmission, input and output material, and personnel are adequate. This review should include not only the computer equipment in the central processing facility but also minicomputers, remote terminals, communications operations, and other peripheral equipment.

Physical Facilities, Personnel, and Security (Cont...)

In reviewing physical security of computer hardware, the auditor should confirm the adequacy of contingency plans for continued processing of critical applications in the event of disruption. This should include provisions for emergency power and backup hardware as well as detailed plans for using the backup equipment and transporting personnel, programs, forms, and data files to an alternate processing location. The auditor should consider the extent to which this plan has been tested to determine the probability of continuing data processing in the event of an emergency.

The auditor must also review the physical security of data files to ensure that (whenever feasible):

- Data and program file libraries are kept by personnel who do not have access to computers and computer programs
- The file libraries are secure
- Computer operations and other personnel do not have unlimited access to the libraries
- Provisions have been made for backup of files (including off-site backup)

When files are normally kept online, the auditor should consider whether they are protected by adequate access authorization controls and whether backup copies are made regularly and are properly identified and labeled. The auditor should exist for program backup files.

Operating Systems Controls

Computer systems are often controlled by operating systems (systems software). Because operating systems usually provide data handling and multi-programming capabilities, file label checking, and many other authorization controls, they are integral to the general controls over computer processing. The auditor should be aware of the controls the operating systems can exercise and should ascertain the extent to which they have been implemented, as well as how they can be bypassed or overridden. The auditor should be aware that personnel who maintain the operating systems, as well as other individuals who are able to modify them, may either intentionally or accidentally cause specific controls within the operating systems to become ineffective.

Hardware Controls

Computer hardware frequently can detect errors related to hardware (as opposed to program) malfunctions. The auditor should be aware of how the installation relies on these hardware controls, how the operating systems use them, and how the detected hardware errors are reported within the installation as well as the procedures for taking corrective action.

REVIEW OF APPLICATION CONTROLS

Before any assessment of processing reliability or integrity in any application can be complete, both the specific application controls and the general controls must be evaluated in their entirety. The auditor therefore has two objectives: determining conformance with standards and approved design, and testing for control weakness.

Conformance with Standards

The first objective is to determine whether the installed applications/systems conform to applicable standards and the latest approved design specifications.

Auditor compliance with this standard provides reasonable assurance that the approved specifications, with all built-in internal controls (e.g., input, processing, output), have been installed as intended, properly documented, and adequately tested.

When the auditor tests data reliability, the test should include examining documentation for selected transactions, testing the clerical accuracy of the entry and summary of transactions, and testing compliance with control procedures. In addition, the auditor may wish to test selected data files to identify possible exception conditions and accuracy of data conversion or capture. If the data files are kept in machine-readable form, the auditor should, where appropriate, use computer-assisted audit techniques in testing them.

Tests for Control Weaknesses

The second objective is to test internal controls and the reliability of the data produced. In addition to evaluating adequacy of controls, such tests may disclose possible weaknesses in the installed applications/systems.

These audits should check the installed applications/systems for adequacy as well as for weaknesses, changed circumstances affecting risk exposure, and so on. Where such weaknesses are found, the auditor's work should stimulate corrective modifications and improve the applications. When conducting tests, the auditor must be aware that there are no guarantees that the application systems will continue to operate in accordance with the latest approved specifications. Adequacy of controls over program changes, program documentation, and operating procedures is therefore critical.

Although auditing for fraud is not the primary objective of audits, the auditor must be alert to the possibility of fraud or other irregularities in computer systems.

THE INSTITUTE OF INTERNAL AUDITORS, INC.
CODE OF ETHICS

INTRODUCTION: Recognizing that ethics are an important consideration in the practice of internal auditing and that the moral principles followed by members of the The institute of Internal Auditors, Inc., should be formalized, the Board of Directors at its regular meeting in New Orleans on December 13, 1968, received and adopted the following resolution:

WHEREAS the members of The Institute of Internal Auditors, Inc., represent the profession of internal auditing; and

WHEREAS managements rely on the profession of internal auditing to assist in the fulfillment of their management stewardship; and

WHEREAS said members must maintain high standards of conduct, honor and character in order to carry on proper and meaningful internal auditing practice.

THEREFORE BE IT RESOLVED that a Code of Ethics be now set forth, outlining the standards of professional behavior for the guidance of each member of The Institute of Internal Auditors, Inc.

In accordance with this resolution, the Board of Directors further approved of the principles set forth.

INTERPRETATION OF PRINCIPLES: The provisions of this Code of Ethics cover basic principles in the various disciplines of internal auditing practice. Members shall realize that individual judgment is required in the application of these principles. They have a responsibility to conduct themselves so that their good faith and integrity should not be open to question. While having due regard for the limit of their technical skills, they will promote the highest possible internal auditing standards to the end of advancing the interest of their company or organization.

ARTICLES:

Members shall have an obligation to exercise honesty, objectivity, and diligence in the performance of their duties and responsibilities.

Members, in holding the trust of their employees, shall exhibit loyalty in all matters pertaining to the affairs of the employer or to whomever they may be rendering a service. However, members shall not knowingly be a part to any illegal or improper activity.

Members shall refrain from entering into any activity which may be in conflict with the interest of their employers or which would prejudice their ability to carry out objectively their duties and responsibilities.

Members shall not accept a fee or a gift from an employee, a client, a customer, or a business associate of their employer without the knowledge and consent of their senior management.

Members shall be prudent in the use of information acquired in the course of their duties. They shall not use confidential information for any personal gain nor in a manner which would be detrimental to the welfare of their employer.

Members, in expressing an opinion, shall use all reasonable care to obtain sufficient factual evidence to warrant such expression. In their reporting, members shall reveal such material facts known to them, which, if not revealed, could either distort the report of the results of operations under review or conceal unlawful practice.

Members shall continually strive for improvement in the proficiency and effectiveness of their service.

Members shall abide by the bylaws and uphold the objectives of The Institute of Internal Auditors, Inc. In the practice of their profession, they shall be ever mindful of their obligation to maintain the high standard of competence, morality, and dignity which The Institute of Internal Auditors, Inc., and its members have established.

APPENDIX B

The "How To" of Writing an Audit Finding

It has been said that "in public or private life, the effective man is the man who can think clearly, say what he means, and put his ideas across on paper. He can clear out verbal brier patches, straighten sentences that have gone awry, and shorten the "distance" from the page to the eyes. His credo is basically Thoreauvian: Simplify, simplify.

But the art of effective and simple communication is not a magic affair that should be delegated to writing magicians. Every person who has to write any kind of report must accept this responsibility himself.

All auditors have an intrinsic responsibility to report on, or more exactly, give a precise presentation of the facts of his or her investigation. Individual findings must stand on their own merit and be reported as self-standing descriptions and narrations.

There are a number of ways to simplify the reporting of audits and the presentation of findings. One might begin by showing (1) what well-developed audit findings have in common, regardless of subject matter. (2) how weaknesses in findings can be identified, (3) how this information can be utilized in writing and further developing findings, and (4) helpful hints for applying this knowledge. The individual attributes of audit findings—how they can be identified and used—will be discussed later. The questions now arise, How do we judge an entire finding, and how can we take advantage of its basic attributes in actually writing better findings and summaries and any other self-contained portion of an audit report?

What are the basic concepts or common denominators? Let me back up a little bit and discuss the elements of any good nonfictional writing. If you were to ask 10 experts how to go about becoming a better writer, you would surely get 10 entirely different answers and methodologies.

But what are some of the basic points that all these experts and many others make in one form or another? They all say that you must:

Organize your thoughts.

Outline your thoughts.

Find the words and sentence structure to convey your thoughts in a concise, grammatical, and persuasive manner.

Practice using these techniques.

Read and study other writer's material.

These points indicate that good, effective findings and report writing (and for that matter, any writing) require a lot of study, practice, analysis, and hard work. You cannot sell a product unless you package it well, but even if you package it attractively, only good contents get repeat orders. Trite but true! Audit packages (reports) are no different.

This section discusses findings in general, their strengths and weaknesses, and elaborates on the first two steps above: (1) organization of thoughts, and (2) outlining of main points. It seems clear, however, that these two steps cannot be successfully taken before you make sure that your analysis of a particular finding indicates that it has a valid point of view a reader can clearly understand. This thought process is really not much different from the generation of an informed opinion on any subject. Is the situation you are describing good, bad, or something in between, and on what do you base your opinion?

So-called good management concepts are really nothing more than a composite of previously established authoritative criteria in any particular business area. Do you rely on them for what you are trying to tell the reader in the finding? What is your overall opinion or point of view? It is unfair and unreliable to have the reader sort out your facts, decide on their relative importance, and conclude what they really mean. That's the job of the auditor who was on the scene.

STRUCTURING THE FINDING

When you have decided whether the situation is good or bad and have substantiated reasons for this decision, the remaining task is to put your thoughts on paper. Put the main point down first, then edit and subdivide the main point if necessary. Show what documentation or statistics you have to prove the point of illustration and what harm, if any, the situation results in. Use the underlying cause as a recommendation for a cure. Of course, all this presupposes that you have done the basic audit work to authenticate an intelligent and useful opinion.

Once you have been able to do this, the rest is a matter of writing tight, semantically attractive sentences, using interesting, active words, spelling them correctly, having them typed neatly, editing the results, and seeing to it that they make good sense. Do all this and you should end up with a clear, and interesting report—provided, once again, that you started with a good examination or audit and one that fully supports your point of view. It should not be surprising to find that those who successfully recognize all the needed attributes of the end product report to begin with (before the audit) usually perform a superior field audit afterwards.

In any event, the schematic description in Figure 1 and the supplementary notes provide helpful "how to" comments regarding findings and the way one actually goes about writing them.

Major Theme

The first paragraph (or two or three, if necessary) represents a summary of the auditor's overall point of view. He (or she) has to decide what he is trying to say about this particular finding and what his composite evaluation is. The first paragraphs of a finding should have the same relation to the rest of the finding that a summary has to the remainder of a report containing a number of findings. One could express it mathematically in this very simple fashion:

$$
\begin{array}{ll}
\text{The first paragraph:} & \text{(is to the)} \\
\text{Rest of the finding} = & \text{(as the)} \\
\text{Summary of the report:} & \text{(is to the)} \\
\text{Entire Report} &
\end{array}
$$

The first paragraph really sets the tone for what follows and serves to give the reader a quick synopsis of the finding, including the recommendation. It should therefore include the five attributes common to all good writing. It is interesting to note that you can usually tell, almost in direct relation to the difficulty you experience in writing the summary paragraph, the number of missing attributes in the whole finding.

Each finding should be self-sustaining and the reader should not have to depend on what was said in previous findings (or subsequent ones) to fully understand the present one. The major theme, in effect, tells the reader to expect explanatory narrative that will support and explain the basis for the overall point of view. The order in which you describe this in the summary paragraph should be the same order in which you later elaborate on them in the body of the finding. It is important to give the reader a sense of tempo, perspective, and orderly sequence, right from the outset.

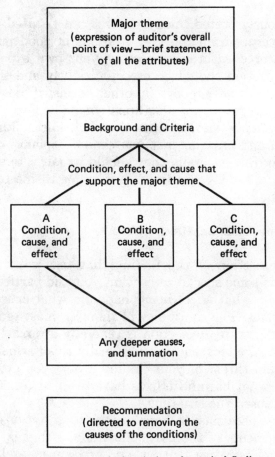

Figure 1.   Schematic description of a typical finding.

Background and Criteria

After you have given the reader your overall point of view and he (or she) can generally picture the entire finding, provide a sense of balance by stepping back a few paces. Discuss the background of the situation and whatever criteria you are measuring the management performance against. This tends to give the narration perspective and indicates what set of values are being considered in this particular situation.

As previously stated, many criteria can be used—stipulated policies, excerpts from the law, citations of good management procedures, or even in certain cases, your own expert opinion. This last criterion should be used judiciously and should have some corroborative support in other forms, if possible. Here again, this paragraph, or paragraphs, should be fairly short. This is not to say, however, that when the whole finding hinges on the background and criteria, that you cannot expound on these to some length. But generally they should be fairly terse, allowing the reader to quickly slip from your major theme to the audit observations.

Description of Condition, Effect, and Cause

This is the section of the finding that tells what you found wrong. (or in some special cases what you find particularly right or well done), what effect it has had, and what caused the specific conditions. The continuity of thought, most report writers find, is enhanced if the section is generally arranged in this order—condition, effect, and cause. Usually this is where you narrate the main thrust of your finding, where you describe what you found, what harmful effects have resulted (or may result), and what caused the situation.

It may be necessary to have different subsections describing different elements of the particular finding; that is, accounting records, administrative controls, and procedures, and the availability of qualified personnel to carry these out. Perhaps program objectives were not being accomplished because resources were expended in the wrong problem area and management was not alerted. The issues may concern money expended needlessly or inappropriately; other resources may have been unnecessarily dissipated or used with only partial effectiveness. Any number of variables can exist.

All the subsections, however, must be related to your overall point of view and be part of the major theme. In each of the subsections it is likely that entire modules of related conditions will come into focus but the basic attributes still remain—condition, effect, and cause; and the analysis of these should be clearly visible.

In this part of the discussion, whole new sets of technical considerations and accounting standards also come into play—sampling techniques (or substitute judgmental analyses, if necessary), physical observations (i.e., inventorying), cost analyses, or even deductive reasoning if that is pertinent and reasonable under the circumstances. One central caution in this area (and this relates primarily to effect) is "Don't overreach." Exercise caution so that you do not create an issue larger than the facts actually warrant.

The sensitive and usually highly judgmental area of cause requires the most penetrating efforts and insights the auditor can call upon. It follows that readers find this to be the most consistently short-changed aspect of the entire evaluation and reporting task. As a minimum effort, the auditor should have dug into the situation deeply enough so that he can generate what we might term a "first level of recommendation," that is, one that is sufficiently detailed or specific enough to enable the recipient of the finding to correct, at the first or working level of management, the correctable conditions cited in the section. The following abstract of a recent letter from a program official to an auditor illustrates quite clearly the importance of cause to a competent report reader:

> ... Your audit has clearly defined several areas of major deficiency at various management levels, in implementing and managing the program during fiscal years 19XX and 19XX, resulting in dilution of the program's intended educational effect. In considering the alternative courses of remedial action available to us, we would benefit greatly from your specific assessment of the ultimate cause of each major deficiency set forth in your report.
>
> As one example, the draft report cites the lack of effective detailed analysis of project proposals prior to approval thereof and a lack of continuing meaningful surveillance, by management, of expenditures during operation of the approved projects. Please tell us whether in your view, those deficiencies stemmed, for instance, from insufficient staff availability (within or beyond our power to augment), lack of appropriate concern and diligence on the part of the organization, inadequacies of state policies or standard practices, misinterpretation or misunderstanding of the letter and spirit of

the federal statute, regulations or guidelines, or inexperience or unaware-
ness of key personnel.

Deeper Causes and Summation

This section is usually the easiest place to analyze the basic causes of the situation. It is also an easy place to overreach. However, in most cases it is very difficult to discuss the deeper causes or the philosophic reasons in a single finding or for that matter in a single audit report. Ordinarily—at least in the audit of a large organization—these can be adequately discussed only in a consolidated report of wide range and scope.

Nevertheless, it is a good place for a summation if you have many subdivisions in the finding. The summation should be very brief and serve only to bring the reader back to your major theme and to recapitulate your point of view. The summation is fairly easy to handle; the main danger is being overrepetitive. The approach can best be illustrated by an adage heard in the military services whenever an officer is to speak before an audience:

Give them a road map.

Tell them where you are going.

Tell them what you want to tell them.

After you tell them, then tell them what it was that you told them.

Recommendation

As previously mentioned, the recommendation will mostly be geared to the working level of management, where specific action can be taken. The recommendations should in all instances be identifiable with the main points in the findings and should, wherever possible, reflect practical solutions to the situations that need improvement or correction.

PUTTING IT DOWN ON PAPER

We have discussed the structure of a finding and its attributes. It may also be useful to talk briefly about the actual mechanics of getting your thoughts on paper. How do you get started?

Many good writers have described their techniques in this time sequence:

1. Jot down cryptic references to all the "bits and pieces" that you want to include in this finding. These shorthand notes serve as useful reminders for including all the sub-points of your finding.

2. After you jot down everything you can think of that may be pertinent to a given finding, decide what your main point of view is. This is a very important step. If you proceed without this overall analysis, you are inviting disjointed narration. One good way to test your point of view is by attempting to write the opening paragraph (major theme) and actually to construct the sentences that describe your evaluation. This effort gives you a quick check as to whether your overall point of view is clearly formed in your mind. If it does not come off smoothly, it is a good bet that more brainstorming is needed.

3. Build the rest of the finding step by step from your bits and pieces and see if they fit into a cohesive pattern, as described above. You can actually frame your finding in a short topic sentence for each of the areas and outline notes under each of the subheadings. It is generally conceded by the writing fraternity that it is quicker, simpler, and more effective in the long run to fully plan and outline your finding (or report) in advance and then to find the words and sentences that will clearly express your views. It is more likely that the findings will then have cohesion and will reflect a tempo of words and ideas that will enable the reader to easily follow your trend of thought.

4. Afterwards, read over what you have written, preferably after it has been typed. This permits a cold, composite (and, it is hoped, dispassionate) opinion of the whole finding.

5. Edit or rewrite if necessary. Scrap the finding, in part or in whole, if it has to be done. Above all, don't become enamored of your own efforts! Not many pieces of writing are perfect.

POINT SHEET

How to Write an Audit Finding

To Be Effective,
  Think Clearly
  Say What You Mean
  Put It on Paper

Effective communication is not a magic affair to be left to a writing magician.

It is every auditor's responsibility to write his or her own report.

Findings ought to be a form of self-contained report.

What Is the Technique? Experts Agree that Good Writers

Organize thoughts.

Decide on overall theme.

Outline thoughts.

Then, find the words and sentence structure to convey evaluations concisely and persuasively.

Practice, practice, practice.

Read and study other writers' materials.

Saying This Differently

Decide on your overall point of view; this is your report—don't ask the reader to determine the relative importance of your points.

Set the stage (background) and cite the criteria or value (what do you base your findings on—stipulated policies, law, good management principles, expert opinion).

Describe what was wrong (or particularly right).

Subdivide the main point, if necessary.

What was the total effect? Be careful at this point not to overreach; don't create an issue larger than the facts warrant.

Cause—this sensitive and usually highly judgmental area requires the most penetrating efforts and insights the auditor can call on (this topic is often short-changed).

Deeper causes and a summation may need a full report of wider range and scope than a single finding; here again, don't overreach.

Recommendations must be identifiable with the main point in your finding and reflect practical solutions for needed improvement.

Putting It Down on Paper (How to get Started in Five Easy Steps)

Jot Down Cryptic References to All the "Bits and Pieces"

These shorthand notes are useful reminders.

Decide on Main Point of View

Again, most important, write the opening paragraph; if this stumps you, rethink it.

Outline the "Bits into a Cohesive Outline

The words and phrases will come easier if this is done *first*.

Read over the Draft

After it is typed, give it a dispassionate appraisal.

Edit Rewrite and Scrap It All If Necessary

Above all, don't become enamored of your own efforts; hardly any first writings are perfect.

APPENDIX C

Summaries: The Bridge Between Audit Effort and Detailed Disclosures

Summaries are considered effective when they successfully compare, in the shortest form possible, *what was* with *what should have been*. A short description should be included of the effect the findings had on programs or organizations, the root causes, and suggestions for related action.

I would like to illustrate how this comparing or balancing process works when related to summarizing the results of internal audits.

Four different types of summaries are frequently used:

1. The Comprehensive/Consolidated Report. This report analyzes underlying concepts, significant findings, and their trends in a series of independent subreports.

2. A Summary of a Single Report. This subreport is part of a comprehensive study but original in its own right.

3. The Summary Paragraph. One or two paragraphs summarize a single finding included in a report.

4. A Briefing Memo. The memo is intended to give the reader a quick synopsis of any of the above. It may also come from other sources, such as trip reports, personal observations, or special analyses.

1. THE COMPREHENSIVE REPORT

This type of report is used to consolidate and highlight broad, underlying factors inherent in a number of other reports. (Each of these other reports, of course, should already have been prepared with summaries. The writing of these summaries is discussed below under heading number 2.) In this document the main ingredient of success is the ability to synthesize the basic elements of managerial and administrative accomplishments that would have constituted good performance.

Comparing "what was" with "what should have been" is the key ingredient. When a writer begins a comprehensive report that summarizes a number of field subreports, he should be prepared, at the outset, to comment on all of the major points related to the scope of the examination covered by these separate reports. The managerial controls and administrative processes concerning these key functions either needed improvement (appropriate recommendations should be stated) or not (the audit disclosed no significant deficiencies). But he cannot be silent *on any of them* and consider the summary complete. There is, of course, no reason why he cannot subdivide any comments pertaining to these principal areas, if needed.

The Writing Process

It might be useful at this point to identify (in a general way) some of the steps in the organization of the subreport material and the thinking process associated with it.

1. Most important is the need for the writer to maintain his focus on what would constitute good performance. This entire report has to be weighed against these initial and basic thoughts.

2. The next logical step is to summarize reported results by the main performance areas.

3. Decide on the total impact of these findings and how much of the total effort in each of the main areas was well done, or something less.

4. Reach a balance, based on demonstrated audit results, as to how well the entire organization performed in relation to what should have been done. Here again, if the audit does not disclose extreme or crystal clear results, a high degree of discretion has to be used in categorizing these results. I am referring to the "middle ground condition." With these it takes adroitness in finding the right words to express an opinion. It isn't always necessary, or desirable, to make flat out statements. Where exceptionally good or poor performance is evident, this may be justified. Here the natural conservativism of auditors is comfortably put aside in the case of these extremes. One could, for example, describe a nonextreme situation in these terms: "Our examination disclosed no significant problems in the procurement and inventory of goods and supplies." Or, "Other than the problems noted in the project approval process, we found no evidence of other administrative weakness."

5. It might also be necessary to trade off good and bad performance in each main functional area. Perhaps the organization did an excellent job in identification of needs, but did a very poor job in the evaluating and monitoring process. Despite the fact management was not looking over its own shoulder sufficiently to see that performance came out well, the end result may have still been very worthwhile; basic objectives may have been met (management will be delighted to read that although problems existed, the job was done.). One might then point out

that an effective monitoring process would help to insure good balanced performance in the future.

6. In describing what was accomplished well and what was not, it is essential to consider why things were not done well. The broader or deeper causes are often discernible or describable only in a comprehensive report. Many regard the full discussion of deep-set causes to be the primary function of this type of in-depth summation. Individual findings, or even entire subreports, often describe only localized superficial causes which may not relate to the broad scene.

7. Another major ingredient would be a discussion of the manner, or efficiency, of overall program operation. This should be considered in the mental balancing process already mentioned; for example, a program or project may have achieved a good part of the desired objectives despite gross inefficiencies in its administrative procedures. The point is that the money wasted in bad application of resources could be better allotted to other aspects of the program, or even to other programs. Uneconomical procurement, extraneous bookkeeping, and inadequate equipment or supplies control are every day examples. It is often useful to relate indirect, or nonprogram findings, to the main program or business objectives. (Did a lack of widgets delay production, for example.)

8. An opinion must also be offered (and it usually fits best in the scope) whether that which was audited was indeed representative of the whole. A report may still be sufficiently noteworthy in its own right, and of great interest to top management, even if it comments meaningfully only on certain aspects of the entire business.

The schematic in Figure 2 may help to illustrate graphically the entire process of writing a comprehensive report. It should be remembered, however, that the report "thinking" process should not be mistaken for the report "writing" procedure. The writing sequence differs from the developmental pattern. Before you draft the very first paragraph, think out the entire report. Then, start writing.

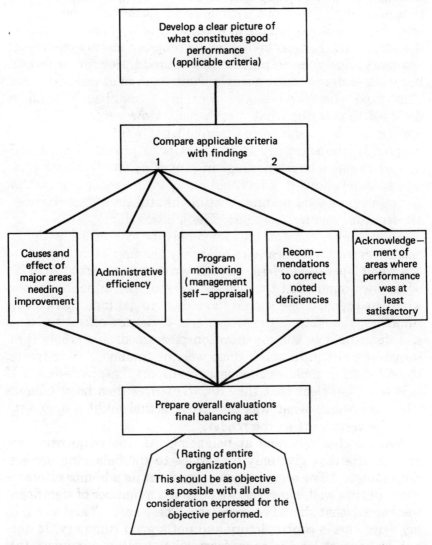

Figure 2. Description of the thought process involved in writing a comprehensive report summary.

2. SUMMARY OF A SINGLE REPORT (SUBREPORT TO A COMPREHENSIVE REPORT)

Many of the basic concepts involved in writing a comprehensive summary apply here, but with some important differences. For one, the scope is much more limited. Normally, it isn't possible to discuss, in depth, aspects of a whole program in only one report summary. But you can narrate how a broad program or project has worked in one state, a single plant, or even at one audit site. This type of report usually contains a number of findings designed to describe what went wrong. However, since findings are not usually designed to describe what went right, the main purpose of the summary of a report is to provide the balance needed to put adverse findings in proper perspective with positive accomplishments. One could easily visualize a report with a fair number of solid findings that might still show that the overall situation was well handled. The job was done!

Additionally, the findings may only be concerned with the need to correct weaknesses in relatively less important aspects of the whole operation. Here, too, the writer has to visualize in his or her own mind what the elements of good performance are and what the organization should have done to get high marks. The summary, therefore, is the proper area to discuss offsetting items and describe how the organization performed as a whole (presumably it did quite well if there were no findings). To reiterate, the audit effort must be adequate to support these statements. If it is less than clear that they do, the writer then must balance (that key word) what was done (the actual audit scope) with what he can report to the reader.

Avoid feeble attempts at balancing. All too frequently, one sees reports that give only lip service to the balancing process. For example, "The organization carried out its administrative responsibilities well. However, we observed a number of significant weaknesses that should be corrected. These are . . ." and so on. In my view, this is contradictory and not a good summary. It does not describe, at least in short form, what positive administrative functions were satisfactorily carried out. A description or analysis of these well-accomplished functions could be supplemented by describing what weak areas slipped by managerial control, and why. That could be the central theme of a report of this type.

Another ineffective type of summary is one that merely contains a consolidated grocery list of the report findings. It usually appears as a short paragraph summarizing each finding, and it frequently fails to give the reader a feel for the entire picture. At its worst, it appears as an almost word-for-word reproduction of the first paragraph of each finding, placed in the front of the report.

The third type of summary of a subreport that misses the target is one where there are no findings and the writer merely gives the organization a one- or two-sentence verbal pat on the back because of this. He does not let the reader know just what it was that earned the organization a good mark. What did it actually do well? How was it able to successfully handle the program objectives and administrative functions with which it was charged? It does not take much to describe this briefly. If the writer feels comfortable to sign off without any findings, he should certainly have enough knowledge to describe what was well done and how and have enough confidence in the audit process to say so.

The schematic in Figure 3 illustrates the comparison process involved in individual report summaries.

3. THE SUMMARY PARAGRAPH

Summarizing a single finding involves a process entirely different from summarizing comprehensive or individual reports. The basic difference is that the writer does not always have to provide a balance in the description of conditions that are not applicable to each particular finding.

The main purpose of the summary of a finding is to present in condensed form (1) the nature of the weakness, (2) the reason for these shortcomings, and (3) the extent of these shortcomings.

This gives the reader a quick idea of what went wrong, why it went wrong, and how wrong it was. Also, what needs to be done to correct things! The writer need not talk about all the other things that were correctly handled in the summary of a finding. That is the function of the full report summary relating to all the findings. Nevertheless, summing up the individual finding is a crucial task because this enables, and forces, the writer to determine what the condition is all about and gives the reader a chance to skip the details if he desires.

4. THE BRIEFING MEMO

This type of writing evokes an entirely new set of summary thoughts. A briefing memo is intended to capsule an entire situation, or an entire organization's performance, in as few words as possible. Conciseness is crucial. The reader, while not knowing the intimate details of what went right and what went wrong, should nevertheless be able to get a strong grasp of whether the overall situation is good or bad, and how good or bad it is. One or two very brief illustrations of the conditions are often very useful.

Good, tight briefing memos are deceptively difficult to write successfully. The writer must first, in his own mind, make all the judgments necessary for the reader to come up to a clear view of the situation. The reader has to immediately feel that he can rely on it, since he lacks knowledge of the intimate details of the situation being discussed. A briefing memo is not useful, or well written, if the reader feels queasy about the summary judgments.

CONCLUSION

In conclusion (and this illustrates a fifth type of summation) the summary is, by any criteria, the most critical element of all reports. It can and should be the focal point of communication between the writer and reader. If done well, the balanced insight

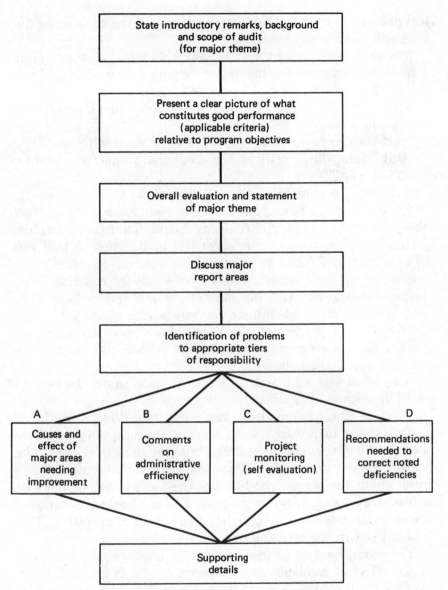

Figure 3. Summary of a single report.

will provide a quick and useful perspective on the supporting details and conditions observed.

I would like to present a short, probably familiar story, call it a fable, to illustrate the matter of "misplaced emphasis." Let's call it "Kropatkin's Law of Socks and Sassing."

Scene: Boy, (any boy) coming home from school, anxious to run out and play.

"Get back in here, young man; I want a word with you!"

"But Mom, Jim's waiting for me," the young boy whines. "Can't it wait?"

"Gregory," replies his mother, "I want you to straighten up, and straighten up fast. You have left your room a mess. How about your homework, eh? And, my friend, don't think I'm forgetting how you sassed your father last night when he told you to turn off the TV and go to bed. That was unforgivable."

Shaken by his mother's anger and suddenly contrite, Greg quickly apologizes. And his mother—as mothers will—quickly hugs her son and sends him on his way with a quick pat.

"Hey Greg, what was all that noise about? Sounded like your mother was chewing you out good," Jim asks as his friend comes running out of the house.

"Oh, Mom was mad because I left my socks under the bed . . . and I've been goofing off on my homework."

"My old man gave me heck last night, too. What a life."

This young man wasn't quite accurate in recapping this little episode. All of the facts were there, but just slightly skewed. The socks were left under the bed as Greg said. But the mother was upset about the general condition of the boy's bedroom, not just a few stray socks. Most important, the mother was infuriated about the manner in which the boy had talked to his father. This was left out in the retelling of the tale.

The moral here, of course, is that one must be ever conscious of the effect of a misplaced or missing emphasis in retelling an event—or summarizing a writing. The whole meaning can be changed or, as in this little example, missed altogether if one is not careful. This process must also be faithfully followed by those of us in the auditing profession.

You have done your work, made your findings, and painstakingly developed your recommendations. Your report is written, and, it is hoped, is a well-balanced presentation.

One major writing chore awaits—boiling it down for the busy, weary executive to read and comprehend. Your skill at distinguishing between "socks and sassing" can sell your professional opinions and observations. A poorly developed digest of even the best report can result in reader misunderstanding. Keep in mind that the report's digest may well be the only part of the report that will be read by the majority of its readers.

Sit back and consider carefully the points you wish to make. Rank their importance. See whether several minor points can be correlated into one single observation—sort those socks! Don't hesitate to stress points that you may believe are obvious. Others may not have your interpretive skills. Be careful, though, about the stress you place on issues of minor substance.

Coming back to Greg for a moment, and applying Kropatkin's Law: He sassed his dad (that's important!). He also didn't do his homework and left his room a mess! That's the way to report on this little episode, or any set of findings.

POINT SHEET

SUMMARIES: THE BRIDGE BETWEEN AUDIT EFFORT AND DETAILED DISCLOSURE

Compare "What Was" With "What Should Have Been." (Four Frequently Used Types)

Comprehensive/consolidated report—analyzes underlying concepts, significant findings, trends in a series of independent subreports.

Single report—a subreport, above, but original in its own right.

Summary of a finding

Briefing memo—quick synopsis of any of the above.

Curt executive note—like "Don't close the plant in Iowa."

Comprehensive Report (Key Ingredient of the Writing Process: A Comparison of "What Was" with "What Should Have Been")

Absolutely imperative to mentally decide what would have constituted good performance.

Summarize main performance areas.

Impact of findings?

Exceptional performance easy (good or bad); "middle ground" needs most attention.

Trade off good and bad areas.

Consider why things were not done well—usually only deep comprehensive reports can do this.

Consider efficiencies—things may have been done well, but at a prohibitive cost.

Consider also—was that which was audited representative of the whole?

Above all—think first, write later.

Single Report

Similar to comprehensive (conceptually), but scope is very much more limited.

Hard to keep balance. Findings not designed to describe what went right; therefore writer must use report summary to do this.

See Figure 3 describing this single report process.

Important caution—avoid feeble attempts at balancing.

Single Finding

Need not have the balance of whole report.

Opening paragraph, however, should be self-standing like a summary of its own.

Briefing Memo

Can take any form but its brevity makes it very hard to keep a proper perspective.

Conclusion

Take particular care here. Don't let it be redundant and an unnecessary restatement of the problem or report. If nothing else, you may inject new unwanted emphases.

APPENDIX D

Internal Controls Self-Appraisal Checklist for the Average Business

1. Physical Entry

Who opens up the office in the morning, who closes up in the evening (and who has keys to doors and files)? Alarm system? What happens at lunch time? In emergencies, such as fire, earthquake, and so on? Do you have backup records?

2. Mail

Who opens mail? Is there a strict routine and register for controlled items? How is cash handled? Is the mail opened promptly or allowed to lie around? The person who opens and records mail should not be responsible for payments or keeping basic books of account. Do you immediately endorse all checks?

3. Receipts

Are they recorded and deposited promptly? There should not be any old items lying around pending a decision as to where they belong. Is there a tickler schedule for regular and repeat items that should be expected? Is there a reminder master list of the types of receipts to enable a staff member to follow up if they are late? Are there some "norms" for general control? Do you use business reply envelopes for customer payments?

4. Expenses

Is there a routine for authenticating checks to be issued? Where is the checkbook? Who reconciles the bank statement? Is it someone other than the signer of the checks? Do you use computer reconciliation with your bank? Is there a petty cash fund? Who has access? Is the routine for paying valid items spelled out in a procedure manual that all can follow strictly? Is there a set method for separating duties in the payment process? What about the amount of the check: Is there a difference in control? Are all blank checks accounted for, including voids? Are checks prenumbered? Are they serially numbered? Are there procurement and receiving documents attached to payments? How are expenses controlled? Do you need special authority for specific amounts or items?

5. Payroll

Are there basic personnel records that support pay scales and authorized hires? Who has the legal authority to put people on the payroll, at what pay scale, or to fire them? What about part-time staff and temporary personnel? How are outside consultants paid? What are the provisions for pension funds, union dues, other deductions, and investments? Who reconciles payroll tax withholding and fills out IRS forms? Are Social Security records accurate?

6. Computer Data and Electronic Transfers

This area requires special attention. Is there a separation of duties among processors, programmers, and others. Who has access to equipment? What happens during illness or vacation? Is data secure from unauthorized scrutiny? Who prepares tax files? What passwords are used? How about use of modem equipment? Is there any use after hours? Do you keep a log of computer time? Is there any leased equipment?

7. Liabilities

Is there a regular schedule of fixed, recurring liabilities? Who makes entries on this record? How are current bills controlled? Are discounts taken where applicable? Where are lawsuits recorded?

8. Securities

Who maintains *physical* control over the documents? Are they in safes? With banks or investment houses? Who verifies? How are they purchased? Who knows the combination to the safe?

9. Other Assets

Where is the cash kept? Fines and miscellaneous receipts? Is every piece of office equipment numbered and its number recorded? Is a routine established for ordering and recording receipt of significant amounts of stationery and office supplies? Is someone in control of the stockroom? What controls shield sensitive small items, such as diskettes, film, etc.?

Index